Creating the Moms Group You've Been Looking For

This book is designed to give general advice on the issues you need to consider when forming a moms group. It is not intended to provide legal or tax advice. Readers in need of detailed advice in these areas are encouraged to consult legal counsel or a certified public accountant.

HEARTS AT HOME® RESOURCE

Creating the Moms Group You've Been Looking For

Your How-To Manual for Connecting with Other Moms

Jill Savage

FOUNDER AND DIRECTOR OF HEARTS AT HOME®

ZONDERVAN™

GRAND RAPIDS, MICHIGAN 49530 USA

We want to hear from you. Please send your comments about this book to us in care of zreview@zondervan.com. Thank you.

ZONDERVAN™

Creating the Moms Group You've Been Looking For
Copyright © 2004 by Jill Savage

Requests for information should be addressed to:
Zondervan, *Grand Rapids, Michigan 49530*

Library of Congress Cataloging-in-Publication Data

Savage, Jill, 1964-
    Creating the moms group you've been looking for : your how-to manual for connecting with other moms / Jill Savage.
        p. cm. — (A Hearts at Home resource)
    Includes bibliographical references.
    ISBN 0-310-25447-7
    1. Church group work with mothers.   I. Title.   II. Series
BV4445.3.S28 2004
259'.085'2—dc22

                                                                                    2003025752

Published in association with Yates & Yates, LLP, Attorneys and Counselors, Suite 1000, Literary Agent, Orange, CA.

Interior design by Michelle Espinoza

Printed in the United States of America

04 05 06 07 08 09 10 /❖ ML/ 10 9 8 7 6 5 4 3 2 1

Contents

How to Get the Most Out of This Book   7

Introduction   9

PART 1: PURPOSE AND VISION

  1. Why Does a Mom Need Professional Affiliations?   13

  2. What Can a Moms Group Affiliation Provide?   16

PART 2: THE OPTIONS AND HOW THEY WORK

  3. Where Do I Start?   23

  4. Playgroups   26

  5. Co-ops   31

  6. Mentoring and Accountability Relationships   37

  7. Small Moms Groups   42

  8. Large Moms Groups   50

  9. What about the Children?   71

PART 3: PRINCIPLES FOR SUCCESSFUL LEADERSHIP

  10. Develop People, Not Programs   81

  11. Pray More Than You Plan   85

  12. Communicate Clearly   97

  13. Cast Vision   103

  14. Build a Leadership Culture   108

  15. Build Communities, Not Committees   113

  16. Facilitate Friendships   117

  17. Handle Conflict Biblically   123

  18. Take Off Your Mask   128

  19. Lean into God   132

  20. Keep the Balance   137

PART 4: THE CHURCH CONNECTION

21. Moms Ministry: An Effective Church Outreach   145

22. What Does This Group Need from Our Church?   149

Appendix A: Professional Resources for Mothers at Home   153

Appendix B: Sample Job Descriptions and Responsibilities   155

Appendix C: Sample Calendars and Schedules   168

Appendix D: Sample Forms   173

Appendix E: Sample Communication   197

Acknowledgments   215

Notes   216

How to Get the Most Out of This Book

AS A MOM LOOKING TO START A GROUP

First, this book will help you discover the type of moms group you are looking for. Then it will give you the steps to create the group you envision. The forms and letters you find in the appendixes are free online at www.jillsavage.org for anyone who purchases this book. They will save you time and assist you in organizing your group.

AS A MOM ALREADY LEADING A GROUP

If you are already leading a moms group, this book will help you evaluate and strengthen various aspects of your group. It will also empower you with tried-and-true leadership principles. You may download the free forms and letters in the appendixes to aid in restructuring areas of the group you are leading (see page 218).

AS A LEADERSHIP CURRICULUM

Part 3 of this book may be used as a leadership curriculum for training moms group leaders. By reserving just 15 minutes of your monthly meeting time for leadership education, you will be able to cover the principles of one chapter a month for a year. It is best for each leader to own a copy of the book so she can read the chapters herself. However, a moms group director can also teach the principles to her leadership team at their monthly team meetings. Free lesson outlines are available online for anyone who purchases this book (see page 218).

AS A CHURCH PASTOR OR LEADER

The last two chapters of this book (part 4) are designed to give vision and encouragement to church leaders. These chapters define the outreach opportunities a moms group can bring to the church and outline logistical needs of the group that the church can help meet. Permission is granted by the publisher to make copies of chapters 21 and 22 to share with a church board, elders, or staff when launching a moms ministry.[1]

Introduction

God certainly has a sense of humor. A girl who didn't have many girlfriends in high school is now leading an international ministry for mothers. I never wanted to mess much with girlfriend relationships. I hung with the guys because they were less likely to form a clique, took conversations at face value, and didn't give each other the silent treatment when they were frustrated. Girl relationships are more complicated!

I have learned, however, that I need girlfriends in my life. I need other women to help me keep perspective and to encourage me on the journey of motherhood. This book represents fourteen years of experience, first starting and leading Mom2Mom, a local moms group, and then starting and leading Hearts at Home, an international organization for women in the profession of motherhood.

Both Mom2Mom and Hearts at Home have seen exponential growth over the years. Mom2Mom began with eight women in my living room and now is a strong moms group that meets in a church and encourages more than 150 moms each week. Hearts at Home began as a one-time conference event in 1994, sponsored by Mom2Mom. Our hope was to provide a one-day conference for mothers at home. This event would feature both keynote speakers and specialty workshops to help moms be the best they could be. We planned for 500 women to attend our event, thinking that was a pretty big goal but feeling capable of handling that number should God send that many women our way. When 1,100 women showed up for that first Hearts at Home conference, we knew God had bigger plans for this ministry than we had ever considered. Today Hearts at Home offers three to four conferences each year and encourages more than 100,000 women annually with conference events, published resources, monthly periodicals, and online resources and connections. The annual Hearts at Home National Conference, held each March in Central Illinois, alone hosts nearly 6,000 moms.

My ten years as leader of Hearts at Home have been a pilgrimage of faith. I've learned lessons of relationship, structure, strategy, and leadership along the way. A teacher at heart, I've always been quick to learn my lessons (many times the hard way!) and then pass on the wisdom to someone else. That's why this book now exists. My prayer is that by my sharing both experience and proven methods, you will be encouraged and equipped to create and lead the moms group you have always wanted.

Part 1

Purpose and Vision

Chapter 1

Why Does a Mom Need Professional Affiliations?

After being a stay-at-home mom for a season, I said to my husband, "I am the only person in my office! Where are my coworkers?" After spending four years in college and then holding down several jobs in the workforce before making the shift to becoming a "Chief Home Officer," I found the isolation of full-time motherhood almost too much to bear.

I was organizationally challenged—always tripping over clutter. My marriage was struggling with the demands of small children taking priority over my husband. Laundry and dishes seemed to be screaming at me all the time, and I felt I could never keep up with the housework. My children were moving through developmental stages that included temper tantrums, pushing the boundaries, bedtime struggles, and more. *Am I the only mom feeling so overwhelmed?* I asked myself. *I must be, because everyone else seems to have it together,* I concluded. Here I was at home with two small children, feeling emotionally depleted much of the time, and thinking, *I went to four years of college for this?* My vision faded, my energies waned, and my self-worth plummeted.

That was 14 years ago. Now after 20 years of marriage and with five children, motherhood is still my profession. My children range from ages 7 to 18, and I have found that the emotions I experience in motherhood are the same emotions most moms experience. I've also learned that I have a huge need in my life to connect with other mothers who are experiencing the same joys and struggles as I am. Over the years I have found my moms groups to be the primary vehicle for connecting with my coworkers, learning about marriage, and sharing the joys as well as the struggles of parenting.

I found myself at home quite by accident. When my husband decided to pursue an advanced degree, our plan included my finding a job teaching music in the local school system. But there were no openings for a music teacher at any grade level in our new community. Because we lived on a college campus, we decided I would offer day care in our home to provide for our family financially. Little did I anticipate that my heart and my life would be changed as I discovered the value of being at home with my children.

We eventually moved again, and I found myself at home with my children in a city where I knew no one. Loneliness set in, and I felt ill-equipped to do this mothering job well.

After meeting a few moms at our new church, I decided to take a risk. I asked eight moms to join me one Wednesday morning to talk about the possibility of having a moms group that would meet weekly. Every mom I invited came that morning. I hired a college student to watch our kids in the basement while we met upstairs and talked about our needs as wives and moms. We decided we would read a book together and talk about one chapter each week. One of the craftier women asked if she could provide a craft project for us every once in a while, and even those of us who were craft-challenged agreed that we would enjoy that on occasion. Another mom offered to organize snacks for the moms and the kids. Little did we know we were on our way to experiencing something that would change our lives forever.

The camaraderie we experienced enriched our lives and helped us realize we were not alone in our profession. The education we received equipped us with knowledge and strategy. The encouragement we provided one another kept us going when we felt like quitting. The friendships that developed extended beyond our Wednesday mornings as we learned how to live life together. The laughter we shared helped us keep our sanity in the midst of the chaos of raising small children. And the tears we shed with one another taught us how to be honest and move beyond surface relationships.

Because coming together once a week was meeting our needs, we couldn't help but share the excitement with other moms. By the end of our first year, our group had grown to 15. By the end of the second year, we had 30 participants, and we no longer fit in my living room. We eventually moved to a church building and saw the group grow to 60 women in the third year. In the years following, the growth continued to more than 150 women attending what we now call Mom2Mom.

Why was there such exponential growth? Because the needs of mothers at home are very real. We no longer live in a society where young mothers are naturally mentored by their mothers or grandmothers. Mom or Grandma may be in the workforce herself and unavailable for one-on-one mentoring and encouragement in the daily struggles a mom faces. Or, in our transient society, they may live too far away to be able to lend such encouragement and assistance. Young women are becoming moms and feeling ill-equipped to handle all that marriage and motherhood require. Many have limited cooking skills. Some struggle to keep a home organized. Still others come into marriage and motherhood with poor interpersonal relationship skills. At the very least, moms face isolation when they are home for a season, because their neighborhoods are empty. Many of their female neighbors are at work outside the home. Moms need a place where they can learn about marriage, motherhood, homemaking, budgeting, and more. They need a place to meet other women who are committed to the profession of motherhood just as they are. Ultimately they need a place where they can be introduced to a God who loves them very much and wants to partner with them in parenthood.

PROFESSIONAL AFFILIATIONS

When I was studying to be a music teacher, I was encouraged to be a part of MENC: Music Educators National Conference. Each time I attended an MENC event, I returned home with new ideas for the classroom, fresh vision for the importance of music education, and an excitement about my at-the-time chosen profession.

In the same way, moms need a professional affiliation that includes events from which they can return home with new ideas, fresh vision for the importance of motherhood, and an excitement about their chosen profession. It's a proven fact that people who are involved in professional development activities are enriched by a sense of "belonging"; they stay in their profession longer. Women who experience a moms group are more likely to be comfortable with their chosen profession of motherhood. They experience a higher level of job satisfaction, and they become better wives and mothers as they are exposed to good resources and teaching about taking care of a family and a home.

When a professional affiliation includes the faith component, a mom is also on her way to understanding the importance of a friendship with God. She experiences an improvement in her quality of life when an eternal perspective is a part of the picture. Most of all, she has the opportunity to hear about a saving relationship with Jesus Christ in a setting that speaks directly to her needs.

FROM MY ♥ TO YOURS

What makes a good moms group? Why did Mom2Mom flourish even when the media told us that being at home was a thing of the past? I believe it comes down to two basic things: addressing felt needs and building solid leadership.

There are many different types of moms groups that you can start or choose to be a part of. Different personalities, different seasons of life, and different needs all factor into choosing which kind of group you want to pursue. Yet the basic components of a healthy group are the same regardless of the size or style. If you are thinking about starting a moms group, my hope is that you will find both encouragement and the practical how-to's to make your vision a reality. If you already are involved in a moms group, my prayer is that you will find fresh vision and new ideas to make your group the best it can be.

Chapter 2

What Can a Moms Group Affiliation Provide?

Each time a moms group meets, certain essential components need to be present. These foundational parts are strategic in nature, designed to meet the needs of a mom who has adjusted her life to meet the needs of her family. Groups may choose to individualize these building blocks, but a group will suffer if it cuts out any one of these, because each building block meets a felt need of mothers. What can a moms group affiliation provide? Let's investigate some foundational elements of a great moms group.

FRIENDSHIP

It's no secret that women tend to be relational. We desire friendships. We want to understand and be understood. A mom who comes to a moms group isn't looking to walk in the door, listen to a speaker, and then walk out the door. On the contrary, she wants to be noticed. She wants someone to take an interest in her. She desires to meet women who know what her life is like. She wants a connection that maintains itself between group meetings. She is looking for friendship.

Friendship doesn't happen simply because a group of people are in the same room at the same time. It happens when a person is intentional in pursuing a relationship. It happens when one mom asks another mom to join her for a peanut butter and jelly sandwich when the group meeting is over. Friendship is one component moms hope to find in a community of mothers.

FUN

For several years I participated in a small group of moms. There were just six of us who gathered together every two weeks. We encouraged one another, shared ideas and homemaking tips, read books together, and prayed with and for one another. But that wasn't all—we also knew how to have fun together!

To celebrate birthdays, we would kidnap the birthday person (with the assistance of her husband and children) and head out for some fun! We'd also use the holidays for an excuse to go on a shopping excursion together, have a slumber party, or go out for dessert after the kids were in bed. Moms need to have girlfriend relationships, and a good moms group can help form those friendships.

Depending on a woman's season of motherhood, she may desire some activities that give her a break from the responsibilities of home. These can be mental health necessities. When my children were preschoolers, I craved an occasional evening away from the house. However, now that my kids are school age, I don't need to get away so often.

A good moms group provides opportunities to temporarily leave the responsibilities of home for a quick reprieve. For years we had an annual slumber party for our Mom2Mom group. One mom would ask her husband and children to go to Grandma's for the night and then open her home up to the moms group. The night would be filled with munchies, movies, games, craft projects, and lots and lots of laughter!

An occasional moms' night out at a movie theater or restaurant is always a big hit. Many groups like to take a trip to a Hearts at Home conference for a weekend getaway that provides a ton of fun!

LEARNING OPPORTUNITIES

Women seem to have an innate desire to learn and to better themselves by improving their skills. Moms groups are a perfect place for this to happen.

Larger, more structured groups may feature a speaker who shares on a specific topic of interest to moms. This workshop setting helps moms to "go to school" to learn more about motherhood, marriage, homemaking, and parenting topics.

Both large and small groups provide an environment to learn from the knowledge and experience of the participating moms. Simply by being in relationship, we glean from the wisdom of other moms whose strengths and experiences are different from ours.

SHARING RESOURCES

Moms groups of any size benefit from the sharing of resources that happens when a group of moms gathers together. Whether it is sharing coupons, favorite books, or recommendations for a good pediatrician, a community of mothers provides a natural opportunity for sharing resources and ideas.

Some moms groups formalize the sharing opportunities by organizing a lending library or coupon table. Other groups enjoy the informal sharing that happens naturally when women talk about mom topics.

Moms can share resources in other ways as well. Members of one moms group in our community took turns providing meals for a family in which the husband had been laid off from work. Another group helped a mom who was adopting a child from Russia fill a suitcase with humanitarian aid items that had been requested by the orphanage. When moms pull together to help one another, both the giver and the receiver are blessed.

RESPITE

Every mom needs a break. Mothering is a 24/7/365 job and will drain us completely if we don't learn the art of self-care. On one hand, being part of a moms group helps a mom keep her emotional fuel tank from hitting empty. Relationships with other moms provide perspective as well as a sense of purpose. On the other hand, being part of a moms group provides respite for the weary mom who just needs to vent and be encouraged to get back in the game.

If the group offers child care, a break once a week or every other week can be a welcome time off from the day-in, day-out care of small children. Not only is this good for moms, but also for their kids. My children looked forward to Wednesdays during their preschool years. What I called Mom2Mom child care, they called "school." They enjoyed the time playing with friends, making crafts, listening to a story, and having a snack.

Another form of respite provided by a moms group is the "break" you get by helping one another. For five years my friend Sue and I alternated Tuesdays off. If it wasn't my day off, it was my day to care for the kids (which really was like a day off too, because the kids played so well together).

Recently, I was speaking at a MOPS group on the topic of marriage. When I talked about the importance of having a date night with one's husband, one brave mom raised her hand and asked how she was supposed to find the money for a babysitter on her limited income. My response was to find another family with children of similar ages and ask that family to trade date nights. She quickly rebutted, "But I have three preschoolers! Who would be interested in trading with me?" Immediately four hands went up in the group. These were four other moms who also had two or three preschoolers. They yelled almost in unison, "I will!" Moms need to connect with other moms to share in having some time off once in a while.

FAITH

One wonderful part of a moms group is being able to meet moms right where they are and then introducing them to or reminding them of the God who loves them right where they are. God becomes very real to a mom who learns about prayer, begins praying about her difficulties, and sees God at work in her life. God comes alive to a mom as she listens to a speaker tell how her struggling marriage was saved when she allowed God to change her heart. Faith becomes very real when you are surrounded by other women who are putting their trust in Jesus Christ.

Most moms groups are an excellent entry point into the church. It is important to remember that not all mothers were raised in a church or are regular church attendees. A moms group is a great place to be introduced to the concept of faith and the hope of a relationship with Jesus Christ. By touching the felt needs of a mother and weaving God's truth and promises into the picture, the stage is set for helping her connect with the God who loves her.

FROM MY ❤ TO YOURS

Meeting the felt needs of mothers is what a moms group is all about. As you think about your own needs and struggles as a mother, assume that most moms would be able to identify with the same emotional highs and lows you experience. When a mom joins a moms group, she needs to be able to find friendship, fun, education, resources, and respite. She also needs a foundation of faith. However, within those components there is much room for creativity! As you include the basic components into your moms group, don't be afraid to personalize the group to meet the needs of the moms in your community.

Part 2

The Options and How They Work

Chapter 3

Where Do I Start?

A lot of initial decisions need to be made when starting a moms group: Where should we meet? What should we do when we're together? What about the kids? How often should we meet? What kind of cost will be involved? Will a church support this? Is there any cost to the church? What kind of leadership is needed? These decisions may seem overwhelming yet nevertheless exciting! Knowing that moms need encouragement on a regular basis is what will keep your vision strong even when challenges come up. I know it worked for me!

But what are the steps to starting a group, and what kind of group best fits you and your community? In this part of the book, I'll help you answer those questions. Chapters 4 through 8 examine several templates for moms groups, starting with informal arrangements and progressing to large, well-structured groups. We'll compare and contrast the groups to help you determine which type best fits your needs, your community, and, if applicable, your church.

To launch our discussion of the various types of groups, let's look at the basic steps to take when starting a new group.

1. PRAY. Pray, pray, and pray some more. The most important part of beginning something new is asking God for direction and wisdom every step of the way. If this is a new concept to you, take extra time to read and absorb chapter 11 so you can better establish a foundation of prayer for this new venture.

2. ASK OTHERS TO JOIN YOU. If you are praying about leading a moms group, personally invite other moms to consider being a part of your group. Set a starting date and begin praying and planning.

If your desire is to start a large group ministry, ask others to join you in praying about it. Set aside several nights to meet and discuss the possibility and to pray together about the start-up details. If you're thinking of a church-sponsored ministry, ask the church leadership to be a part of this process.

After praying together several times, ask other moms if they will commit to lead or participate in the group. This core group will be the foundation for establishing and growing a larger group.

3. ARE YOU PRAYING? God knows what his plan is for this group—do you trust his plan more than yours? Is he in the driver's seat, or are you still vying for the steering wheel? Keep praying!

4. DETERMINE THE STYLE OF THE GROUP. What kind of programming do you envision? Will the group meet weekly, every two weeks, or monthly? What kind of child care, if any, will be needed? (See chapter 9 for a discussion of child-care options.) Will the group be "open" or "closed"? Most small groups are considered closed. In a closed group, the women commit to stay together for a predetermined season of time, usually one or two years. The group is not "open to the public" and remains small, intimate, and intentional about building close, trusting, honest relationships. Most larger groups are considered open, meaning they are open for any mom to attend; the group's vision foresees intentional growth both in size and depth of relationship.

5. PRAY SOME MORE—SEEK GOD'S DIRECTION IN ALL DECISIONS. God cares about all the details of your new ministry venture. Don't neglect praying about the little details as well as the big decisions.

6. DETERMINE INITIAL LEADERSHIP NEEDS. To launch your group, what leaders need to be in place? What permissions, if any, need to be secured from church leadership to proceed? What facility requirements do you have?

7. STILL PRAYING? Don't get ahead of God. Trust God to show you every step of the way and to bring together the necessary leadership team. If a team is not coming together in the time frame you have set, be willing to wait if necessary. The best place to be is right in the middle of God's will. Wait on him.

8. DETERMINE A LAUNCH DATE. Your launch date may be 2 months away, or it may be 12 to 18 months out. Regardless of when your launch date is, continue meeting with your leaders on a monthly basis to pray together, cast vision, get organized, and build relationship.

9. PREPARE INITIAL MARKETING EFFORTS. If you are starting a moms group, moms need to know about it. Get the word out by putting a public service announcement in the local newspaper, a notice on the bulletin board in the children's area of the public library, and announcements in church bulletins and newsletters. Place brochures or post announcements in pediatrician and obstetrician/gynecologist waiting rooms. Don't forget word of mouth; your team members are a great tool for spreading the word.

10. STAY ON YOUR KNEES. Ask God to keep you balanced in the time you are giving to this group. If you are consumed with responsibilities to the neglect of your family, it's a sure sign you need more help to spread out the workload.

11. CELEBRATE WITH YOUR TEAM AFTER YOUR FIRST MEETING. Most likely the moms who have shared your vision along the way will have put a lot of time and effort into the launch of this ministry. Celebrate with your launch team over a piece of pie at your favorite restaurant the night after the group meets for the first time.

FROM MY ❤ TO YOURS

When God gives you a vision to encourage other moms, he is sending you on an exciting adventure. Be prepared to learn a lot about yourself along the way. You will be stretched and challenged in ways you could never imagine. Your character will be honed, your patience will be tested, and you will learn about God and his faithfulness in a very real way. Don't run from these learning opportunities; instead, cherish them as wonderful ways to expand your abilities. I would never trade my years of leading our moms group. I am a different person today because of the women God allowed me to get to know through the moms group experience. He will provide an exciting adventure for you as well!

Chapter 4

Playgroups

Playgroups are relatively simple moms groups to organize. Invariably when moms get together, even in an informal setting, they are sure to discuss the subjects that most moms struggle with. Although moms in organized playgroups don't experience a true respite from the responsibilities of taking care of children, as they would with child care available, a sense of camaraderie is experienced and the foundations of friendships are laid as the moms gather on a regular basis to visit and let their children play together.

TYPES OF GROUPS

Playgroups usually fall into one of three program categories.

Some moms enjoy just getting the kids together weekly or every other week at one another's home and letting their children play under their watchful eyes. This style of group—unstructured play—allows mothers to visit together while the kids play together.

Other groups offer a bit more structure with parent-child activities, such as simple craft projects, story times, or games.

Still other groups like to offer "get-out-of-the-house" activities that are more like field trips for moms and kids. They may visit the zoo, children's museum, park, or McDonald's playland for their regular gatherings.

JULI'S STORY

After leaving full-time work to stay at home with my two boys, I felt that I needed to have some connection with other moms who were doing the same thing. I asked a few acquaintances to join me in a playgroup, and those moms in turn asked a few more moms. This first playgroup provided companionship but not true friendship, because we seemed to have very little in common.

After that group disbanded, I hand-selected my next playgroup. I invited three moms I knew from my church. Two of the moms had two preschool-age children, and one mom was expecting her second child. The group has been meeting each Monday morning for over a year now. We rotate homes each week, and the hostess makes lunch for everybody (lunch for both moms and kids is simple, kid-friendly food like chicken nuggets and tater tots!). After lunch everyone heads home for nap time.

Occasionally we do a holiday activity together like baking Christmas cookies with the kids in December. Usually, however, our playgroup agenda is simple: The kids play and the moms visit. This playgroup has not only provided companionship but true friendships that encourage me in the profession of motherhood.

START-UP CONSIDERATIONS

If a playgroup is the style of group you are looking for, where do you start? What do you do to make a successful group? It's really not difficult to organize a playgroup. Here are some ideas:

DETERMINE THE AGES OF CHILDREN YOU DESIRE TO INCLUDE. This will probably be based on the ages of your own children. What range are you looking for? Just infants? Maybe toddlers? Is your primary age range preschoolers between the ages of 3 and 5? Is it okay for moms to bring siblings along who don't fall into the playgroup age range?

DETERMINE THE SIZE OF YOUR GROUP. Most successful playgroups have between 5 and 10 parent participants. If each mom has only 1 child, 5 to 10 children will play together at each session. However, if some of the moms have 2 or more children, this could mean 15 to 20 children playing at each gathering. Be sure you can keep things under control and safe for all involved.

DETERMINE THE DAY AND TIME THAT WORK WELL FOR YOU. Most playgroups meet in the mornings simply because many toddlers and preschoolers take naps in the afternoon.

DETERMINE THE LOCATION. Do you want to rotate homes? Would you prefer to host the group in your home each week? Is there a park or other central location you may want to consider?

DETERMINE THE STYLE OF GROUP YOU WANT TO HAVE. Do you want to meet and let the moms visit while the children play? Would you like to have parent-child activities planned each time to foster interaction? Some groups prefer to be field trip oriented, planning their times around trips to the zoo, children's museum, park, swimming pool, etc. Other groups like to weave a faith lesson into their time together with an object lesson, story, or short devotional.

DETERMINE YOUR APPROACH TO PLANNING ACTIVITIES. Some groups allow the mom who is hosting the group at her home to determine the activity for that week. Other groups select an activity coordinator to put together a schedule of activities or field trips.

Still other groups plan activities by consensus. Trips or activities can be planned from one week to the next or one month at a time; or a six- to nine-month schedule can be created and followed.

DETERMINE WHETHER FOOD WILL BE A PART OF THE GROUP. You'll need to decide if you want to offer a snack each time. If so, will the members rotate this responsibility? Is "kid food" different from "mom food," or is the snack something everyone can enjoy?

DETERMINE WHETHER YOU WANT TO ADVERTISE YOUR GROUP TO THE GENERAL PUBLIC OR INVITE MOMS TO JOIN YOU. If you invite moms to join you, you can be a bit more selective about whom your children will be playing with. You may want to have a playgroup only with other moms from your church, which will help build church relationships. However, if you are new to the community or even new to motherhood and don't know too many mothers, you may consider some general advertising. You can create posters on your computer and post them in places where moms will see them: children's department at the library, pediatrician's office, children's secondhand store, etc. When you begin to invite other moms or handle inquiries from the advertising you have done, make sure you know the basic details of how your group will be organized. If you are clear about your goals and the style of the group, it will help other parents determine if your group will be a good fit for them.

DETERMINE WHETHER THE GROUP WILL BE OPEN OR CLOSED. Can other mothers invite friends to come to the group on occasion without asking permission? Can another mom be added to the group with the group's general consent? At what point, if any, is the group at maximum capacity and unable to accommodate other moms and children?

GROUP GUIDELINES

As you start up, give the group some basic information and guidelines. You don't want to burden the group with rules, but some general guidelines will help keep conflict and confusion to a minimum. At your first meeting it may be helpful to have a one-page information sheet that has the name of the group (be creative—pick something like "Preschool Pals" or "Kids Korner"), the names, addresses, phone numbers, and email addresses of the moms and children participating, the dates you will meet for the next six to nine months, a snack rotation schedule, and some basic guidelines to help the group work well together. Here are some suggested principles you may put in writing:

- If you or your child has had a fever or a green-mucous runny nose within the past 24 hours, please do not participate in playgroup.
- Each time the playgroup meets, remind your children of your expectations for their good behavior and the importance of sharing and being kind. Use this as a learning environment for helping your child develop social skills.

- Please keep an eye on your child's behavior and address behavior issues as needed.
- If you feel frustrated or uncomfortable with another mom, please address the conflict in a biblical manner. Don't talk to anyone else about the problem. Instead, follow the principles of Matthew 18 and go directly to the mom with whom you are struggling, asking her to sort through the issue with you. (See chapter 17.)
- Have fun and enjoy the time together!

QUICK VIEW OF A PLAYGROUP

Style of group:	Open or closed
Meets:	Weekly or every two weeks
Time of day:	Usually morning
Type of program:	Three types of groups are successful: 1. No program at all 2. Simple, planned parent-child activities 3. Planned field trips
Sample meeting:	Moms gather at a set time and location to visit while their children play together.
Cost to moms:	None; however, the meeting place often rotates with each mom taking a turn hosting the group. If the group is field trip based, a cost for entrance fees may be incurred. If snacks are provided, a cost of providing the snack on rotation may also be incurred.
Cost to church:	None
Child care:	Not needed
Leadership required:	Playgroup coordinator
Additional leadership possibilities:	Food coordinator, activity coordinator, field trip researcher, devotional coordinator

FROM MY ❤ TO YOURS

The first moms group I ever experienced was a playgroup. I felt inexperienced as a mom and quite honestly found my days long and laborious with my 18-month-old daughter. I discovered that just by being with other moms, I experienced new energy in my mothering. Those other moms didn't realize how much I was watching them as they interacted with their children. My playgroup experience gave me vision for my job as a mother. If this is the moms group you are longing for, I know you will benefit greatly from being with other moms on a regular basis!

Chapter 5

Co-ops

For years Sue and I traded days off. One Tuesday was my day off and the next Tuesday was hers. We used our days off to go to lunch with our husbands, shop without the kids, work on redecorating projects, or even take naps or read books if that's what we wanted to do! Our days off were completely ours to do whatever we felt like doing.

Sue's second child and my third child were born within four weeks of each other. Our friendship blossomed during that year as we sat in each other's living rooms, rocking and nursing our babies and chatting away. As the kids entered their second year, we came up with the idea of trading days off. Our older children were in school, and now we had toddlers who were home by themselves all day. Why not give each other a break and let the kids play together once a week? We picked a day, determined the rotation, and put our idea into motion.

As the kids got older, they could hardly wait for their play day. At our house, Erica would ask, "Is this a Nick day?" At Sue's house, Nick would ask, "Is this an Erica day?" We continued the exchange for four years, all the way through their preschool year when we would do the exchange after they were home from school.

Never once did Sue and I use the term "co-op" when we referred to our agreement, but that's exactly what we had: a day-off co-op. A co-op is formed when moms decide to share a service or activity between or among themselves without the exchange of money. The pay is with time rather than money. Below are the benefits we discovered participating in a child-care co-op.

- I was always more comfortable leaving my child with another mother than with a teenage babysitter.
- We had more time than money.
- By taking the children to another home, our home remained available for finishing a project or just spending time at home without children.
- Our children made friends and enjoyed playing together.
- We were able to exchange for longer periods of time than we could have afforded if we had paid a sitter.

TYPES OF CO-OPS

There are many types of co-ops in which moms can participate. You may want to organize a co-op based on your needs in your current season of motherhood. Following are some other co-op ideas.

DATE NIGHT CO-OP

With no family in town and little money to pay a babysitter, my husband, Mark, and I found it necessary to arrange a co-op with another couple to give us time together without children (in other words, so we could have a date!). We asked another couple if they would be willing to devote every Saturday afternoon and evening to a babysitting exchange. We loved having a regularly scheduled time to go out, and it enriched our marriage. We also enjoyed an extended time together, sometimes even six to eight hours. We never could have afforded a sitter for that long, but we certainly could return the favor by caring for the other couple's children for the same amount of time the next week.

One couple we know did an overnight exchange with another couple every Friday night for several years. This gave them an entire night in their home without children twice a month. Their kids loved being with their friends, and even the parents who were watching the kids found they had great communication and project time, because the two families of kids entertained one another and played well together. It was a win-win situation for everyone!

COOKING CO-OP

Some moms band together to tackle family meals in bulk. By devoting one day a month to cooking freezer meals, these moms reduce the hassle and increase the fun of meal preparation. A cooking co-op not only saves time in the daily task of making meals, but it saves money by reducing the temptation to eat out. It also saves money because you buy in bulk and shop with a plan. Here are some tips for making a cooking co-op work.

- Find a friend whose family has similar food preferences as your family.
- Select 10–15 recipes that are freezer friendly. Together make double, triple, or quadruple of each recipe for each family.
- Don't forget the simplicity of browning, seasoning, and freezing pounds of hamburger at a time that can be used for chili, tacos, and sloppy joes at a moment's notice.
- Select a day to shop and another day to cook each month. For instance, you might want to say that the fourth Thursday and Friday of every month are your shopping and meal preparation days.
- Arrange for child care for the children. Also making arrangements with your husband to eat out on your cooking day! You'll be exhausted after being on your feet in the kitchen all day.

- Select the home with the largest kitchen for your meal preparation day.
- Put on music, don an apron, and start cooking!

For more ideas on getting a cooking co-op started, check out www.30daygourmet.com and www.cookingamongfriends.com.

KIM'S STORY

I don't enjoy the meal-making responsibilities of motherhood. I used to find myself waiting too late to start dinner and rushing to find something to throw together for my family. When my friend Kate asked me if I would be interested in doing once-a-month cooking with her, I jumped at the chance!

Kate and I go to breakfast together one Thursday each month to plan our menus for the next cooking day. After determining our freezer meal menus, we create a master shopping list. We then head to the store to shop together for the needed ingredients for our meals. We each pay for half of the grocery bill. Then we take our items to Kate's house (she has the bigger kitchen!) to get ready for our cooking day on Friday. Kate's kids are in school, so she doesn't have to worry about a sitter. My children, however, are preschoolers, so I arrange for a sitter for both days. We start early Friday morning browning meat and preparing the ingredients for our recipes. Then we begin assembling our freezer meals. We wash the dishes together throughout the day. By the end of the day we not only have 15 to 20 freezer meals, but we have enjoyed a lot of laughter and wonderful camaraderie that will stay with us for years to come.

CLEANING CO-OP

Although it takes some humility to allow someone to see your dirty bathroom, there is great energy and momentum when you clean with a friend or a group of friends. Some moms have found that this kind of co-op helps motivate them and helps them to enjoy cleaning their home. The benefits include:

- The job is done in half the time. Some moms have found that if they co-op with a friend, they can clean one house in the morning and the other in the afternoon.
- The conversation that can happen while you dust or mop can be spontaneous and fun.
- You are more likely to stay on task and not get sidetracked when a friend is helping. You may even consider not answering the phone on your cleaning day.

- When you have a schedule to keep with a friend, it helps you settle into a routine that benefits everyone.
- You may want to consider adding laundry to the co-op. Folding a load of laundry will go twice as fast with a friend, the conversation will be rich, and you will be able to get back to cleaning faster.
- Lunch out together on cleaning day may serve as a reward for your hard work.

BABYSITTING CO-OP

An organized babysitting co-op can include as few as 4 or 5 families or be as large as 40 to 50 families (often in a church or neighborhood setting). Certainly larger co-ops will take more organization, but the basics of a babysitting co-op are very simple.

Co-op members agree to share babysitting among themselves without the exchange of money. Some co-ops choose to use coupons or chips to "pay" one another for sitting. Other co-ops choose to have a secretary keep track of credits earned and spent. Regardless of which way you choose to handle the "pay," most co-ops start their members with an initial amount of credit, coupons, or chips. This way they are able to use the co-op right from the beginning, but they have to care for someone else's children if they are to continue benefiting from the co-op after using their initial allowance.

When organizing a babysitting co-op, you have to set up a scale for "pay." Here is a suggestion:

- 2 chips per child per hour (can be figured to the half hour)
- 1 chip per child for every meal served
- 1 chip per child per hour for overnight care

The leadership needed for a co-op will depend on how you organize the group. The co-op coordinator will usually carry the responsibility of orienting new members to the co-op, distributing the initial coupons or chips, evaluating the co-op's effectiveness by surveying the participants every three to six months, and leading meetings as needed. A secretary usually keeps the roster up-to-date. She may also keep track of credits earned and spent. You most likely will want to offer extra chips for those who carry leadership positions in the co-op. For instance, you may offer 10 to 15 extra chips each month for the coordinator and secretary. At the very minimum, an annual meeting should be held to evaluate and select new leaders or affirm current leaders each year.

If you organize a co-op, make sure you clearly communicate information and expectations. Create a roster of all those in the co-op, including parents' names, addresses, phone numbers, email addresses, and children's names and ages.

START-UP GUIDELINES

When setting expectations, you may want to put some of the following suggested principles in writing.

- If you or your child has had a fever or a green-mucous runny nose within the past 24 hours, please do not agree to watch someone's children or expect someone to watch your child.
- Each time your children go to someone's home, remind them of your expectations for good behavior and the importance of sharing and being kind. Use this as a learning environment for helping your children develop social skills.
- Keep open, honest communication with the families with whom you co-op. If there is communication about your child's misbehavior, don't take it personally; rather, look at it as an opportunity for your child to learn and grow. Don't hesitate to give your children consequences for misbehavior in your absence. This will help them learn that they need to respect the authority of whoever is caring for them.
- If you feel frustrated or uncomfortable with another mom or family, please address the conflict in a biblical manner. Don't talk to anyone else about the problem. Instead, follow Matthew 18 and go directly to the parent with whom you are struggling, asking him or her to sort through the issue with you (see chapter 17). If that interaction does not go well, ask for assistance from the co-op coordinator.
- Have fun and enjoy the benefits of taking care of yourself and your marriage!

QUICK VIEW OF A CO-OP

Style of group:	Open or closed
Meets:	As needed
Time of day:	Anytime
Type of program:	No formal program
Sample meeting:	No formal meeting
Cost to moms:	There is no financial cost with a co-op. You "pay" by exchanging time.
Cost to church:	None
Child care:	All exchanged
Leadership required:	Babysitting co-op: coordinator, secretary

Other co-ops: no leadership needed, just someone brave enough to ask another mom to join her in doing some task together on a regular basis.

FROM MY ❤ TO YOURS

I am amazed at the number of moms who complain about not getting anything accomplished, not having any time for themselves, and not having money to pay a babysitter yet do nothing about it. Every mom needs a community of mothers on whom she can depend. In our transient society in which many of us do not live near extended family, we have to create our own network of relationships to call upon when a need arises. Rather than being reactive and stressing out when you need help, be proactive by putting relationships and structures in place that will help you enjoy to the fullest the season of raising children!

Chapter 6

Mentoring and Accountability Relationships

Becky approached me one Sunday after church. A new mom trying to navigate the journey of parenthood, she wanted to keep her spiritual life growing but didn't know how. She was also discovering that keeping her marriage a priority was a challenge with a baby consuming her time and energy. "Would you be willing to meet with me one morning each week to help me learn to be a wife and mother?" she asked while working hard not to break into tears.

Becky and I agreed to meet at 6:00 A.M. on Thursday mornings for six months. Because her husband left for work early, we met in her living room, taking advantage of the quiet before her baby awoke in the morning. My husband needed to leave the house by 7:30 A.M. to go to work, so we had a little over an hour each week before I returned home to care for my children.

I listened a lot during those first few weeks as Becky shared her heart. I tried to determine what needs she had and how to best meet those needs in our time each week. We decided to read the book of Philippians together and discuss personal applications each week. We then studied together the book *Experiencing God*[2] before we concluded our meetings six months later.

Those lessons from our studies will always stay with us. Yet I was surprised that Becky later told me that what most influenced her then was seeing that I, also, didn't always have my act together. My honest sharing helped her realize that we all have struggles. It brought perspective to her and helped her to feel "normal." God's truth had changed my heart in my marriage, so when I saw Becky dealing with the same attitudes I had harbored, I could share God's truth from a personal perspective. When she struggled as a parent, I could discuss what Bible verses had meant the most to me when I faced those same challenges. This gave her hope. And she was encouraged as I talked about and modeled some "next steps" she could take in her journey.

While mentoring and accountability relationships may not be considered an actual moms group, many women seek out this kind of encouragement. Young moms benefit from one-on-one mentoring relationships that allow them to glean from more mature moms who have experienced the seasons of motherhood they are now passing through. These relationships can also provide accountability for women who want to grow deeper spiritually.

Donna Otto discusses the importance of mentoring in her book *Mentors for Mothers:* "A younger woman is given the incredible opportunity to learn from a woman who has walked where she is walking . . . who is willing to open her heart and lay her life experience before the younger woman, and who has survived but has not 'arrived.'"[3] Most moms crave a relationship that helps them succeed in the season they are in or prepares them for the next season of marriage or parenting. Mentoring relationships are an excellent format for addressing a mother's needs, and they can be either formal or informal.

INFORMAL RELATIONSHIPS

Informal mentoring relationships would more likely be called friendships. My friend Doris mentored me through the process of parenting a high schooler; her son was one year older than my daughter. I watched Doris as her son got his driver's license, went to the prom, and graduated from high school, and in doing so, I felt more prepared when I faced those transitions myself. I learned how to find a balance between holding on and letting go by watching her go through the process. We would never have called our friendship a mentoring relationship, but in reality it was.

JEANIE'S STORY

One Sunday as I was reading the church bulletin, I came across an announcement of the launch of a new mentoring ministry. I was one of 10 women who attended the informational meeting to consider being a mentor. I decided to make myself available and was matched up with a young woman who was looking for encouragement.

For the past two years, we have worked to meet every other week for lunch. I try to touch base with her by phone weekly and send her occasional notes of encouragement. The areas in which she needs the most encouragement is learning how to forgive and how to trust God, and I've tried to steer our conversations in that direction. She has been very self-focused, so I have arranged service projects we can do together to help her place her focus on others. In the midst of encouraging her, I have found that the mentoring experience has stretched me in ways I never could have imagined.

FORMAL ARRANGEMENTS

Other mentoring relationships have a more formal arrangement. This is what Becky and I experienced. Formal mentoring relationships start when one mom approaches another and asks her to teach her from her own experience. Sometimes the mentor is older in age; sometimes she is older in experience. The Bible talks about this in Titus 2:3–5: "Teach the older women to be reverent in the way they live, not to be slanderers or addicted to much wine, but to teach what is good. Then they can train the younger women to love their husbands and children, to be self-controlled and pure, to be busy at home, to be kind, and to be subject to their husbands, so that no one will malign the word of God."

Some moms desire accountability in a mentoring relationship. One mom told me that she had realized that she had a very critical spirit. Her criticism was tearing apart her marriage and damaging her children. She asked a woman to mentor her and hold her accountable. The mere knowledge that someone was watching and asking tough questions helped her to be cognizant of her behavior and make needed changes. Accountability can also be mutual if that is established at the beginning of the relationship. In making accountability mutual, you are giving one another permission to ask tough questions, such as, How is your marriage *really?* What sin do you struggle with the most? What do you feel God is asking you to learn? These honest, sharing relationships also allow two people the opportunity to become prayer partners. As you share your difficulties, you learn how to pray for one another.

FINDING A MENTOR

The hardest part of finding a mentoring relationship is finding a mentor. Many older women don't feel they have anything to offer a younger mom. They underestimate the value of their experience. They don't understand the importance of sharing honestly from their own struggles, challenges, mistakes, and victories to help another mom flourish in marriage, motherhood, friendships, homemaking, and more.

Where can you find a mentor? Begin by watching other women. If you identify traits in another woman that you desire for yourself, take a second look. What women do you admire? Who have you seen in action as a woman of integrity and character? Search for a woman who is Christ-centered even in the midst of difficulties. You can also ask your pastor or director of women's ministries for recommendations.

When you approach another mom and ask her to mentor you, encourage her by explaining that you are not looking for great wisdom. Instead, you are looking for one who understands the journey and has navigated it before. A good mentor is one who seeks to be like Jesus but isn't afraid to talk about the times she has blown it. You might also suggest that you agree to commit to meet for only three to six months, after which you would both evaluate your desire to continue or change direction.

Remember that you can be a mentor to someone else too. There is always someone two steps behind you who can benefit from your wisdom, experience, and encouragement. Don't negate what you can offer, because in the giving, you will be sure to receive much as well.

QUICK VIEW OF A MENTORING RELATIONSHIP

Type of group:	Mentoring relationship
Style of group:	Closed
Meets:	Weekly, every other week, or even monthly
Time of day:	Anytime
Type of program:	No program is needed, but often a curriculum or study is used
Sample meeting:	Most mentoring pairs meet 1 to 2 hours per session for discussion and prayer
Cost to moms:	Child care if paid sitter is needed
Curriculum:	A workbook or book may be purchased
Cost to church:	None
Child care:	Arranged individually
Leadership required:	A mentor

FROM MY ♥ TO YOURS

I have had the benefit of sharing in both formal and informal mentoring relationships, and my life is richer because of those experiences. When we're honest and vulnerable about our own struggles, we are on our way to learning more about ourselves and more about God. I encourage you to find a mentor who will share God's truth with you when you need it. Be a mentor who will do the same. If the relationship is based on the foundation of Jesus Christ, it will bless both of you for years to come.

SUGGESTED CURRICULUM AND RESOURCES FOR MENTORING

Henry Blackaby, *Experiencing God Workbook*
Stormie Omartian, *The Power of a Praying Parent*
Stormie Omartian, *The Power of a Praying Wife*

Donna Otto, *Between Women of God*
Donna Otto, *Mentors for Moms*
Martha Peace, *The Excellent Wife*
Allie Pleiter, *Becoming a Chief Home Officer*
Jill Savage, *Professionalizing Motherhood*
Jill Savage, *Is There Really Sex after Kids?*

Chapter 7

Small Moms Groups

Julie started our afternoon with prayer, and then we enjoyed pie and coffee as we sat in her comfortable family room. For 15 minutes, the six of us casually conversed about kids' activities, unexpected home repairs, and the challenges of living on one income. After clearing away the dishes and giving refills on coffee, Julie brought focus to our gathering. We had agreed to read together *The Power of a Praying Parent,*[4] and today we were discussing chapter 7. She asked us what passages we had highlighted, and for the next 30 minutes we talked about our discoveries. Julie further asked what each of us felt God was really pressing into us as a result of reading the chapter. Did he bring a verse of the Bible alive for us? Did he challenge us to take an action step? Our conversation was both encouraging and challenging, as we learned from one another and took the information to a deeper, more personal level.

In bringing our discussion to a close, Julie transitioned into the importance of being there for one another. She set a date for us to serve one of our group members by helping her clean her house in preparation for her daughter's graduation open house. We all agreed to be there, looking forward to the opportunity but also knowing that when we had a need, the group would be available to help us. Then Julie gave us each 5 minutes to share what was going on in our lives. What joys had we experienced? What challenges were we facing? How could we be praying for one another?

We closed our time with prayer, each person praying for the woman to her right. As I left that afternoon, I felt filled up relationally. I knew I wasn't alone in the pilgrimage of life. And I was encouraged to grow in my faith and in my family relationships.

The small group experience can offer rich relationships as well as encouragement and accountability. Organizationally, it requires simple leadership and doesn't call for a lot of preparation. Many small groups meet in members' homes. When the group meets in a particular home, usually the dad or a babysitter keeps the hostess's children in another part of the home. Groups may also choose to meet at a restaurant, church, or library conference room.

TYPES OF GROUPS

CLOSED GROUPS

A small moms group is often a great format when you are looking for depth of relationship as well as meaty discussion. Most small moms groups start by invitation and continue in a "closed" format not open to women dropping in uninvited. In the initial invitation, the leader considers each woman's personality, needs, maturity level, and faith journey as she looks to pull together a cohesive group of women who share a common affinity for one another.

In most small groups it takes one to two years for in-depth relationships to be formed. However, it is wise to ask everyone for an initial six-month commitment. At the end of that time, the members can evaluate whether they want to extend the commitment for a longer season. (Is this group working for you? Is it meeting your needs? Can you make it a priority for the next year?) Some groups operate with a "birthing" mind-set, encouraging some members to start and nurture new groups after an initial 18- to 24-month experience. Other groups choose to meet together for years, allowing the group to change as the women enter into different life seasons.

One group I know met every other week when members were all mothers of preschoolers. They structured their discussions around a theme or a book they agreed to read. As their children began school and some of the moms returned to part-time work, they moved to a monthly, less formal gathering. Now some 10 years later, the group no longer meets monthly but schedules an annual dinner at which they "catch up" and preserve their long-term relationships.

OPEN GROUPS

Other small groups require little commitment and have an "open" format. Their members come when they can and bring friends or new members as they desire. The benefit of this is its appeal to someone who hesitates to commit. It also allows the group to be open to whomever God may bring along to enjoy the gatherings. A drawback is the possibility of the group quickly burgeoning. Also, when group members come and go, group honesty and vulnerability is limited, because trust can't be built easily.

MOMS IN TOUCH

If prayer is a priority for you, you may consider starting a Moms In Touch group. Moms In Touch is an international ministry that encourages mothers whose children attend the same school to pray for their children and that particular school. Groups meet just one hour each week, and prayer is the only item on the agenda. The leadership role is simple, and the Moms In Touch ministry equips you to do the job. The ministry offers both state and national leadership support to local group leaders. For more information on Moms In Touch, contact them at www.MomsInTouch.org.

KAREN'S STORY

Four years ago my friend Carmon and I decided to plan an informal get-together for a few friends around the holidays. We were all at-home moms knee-deep in diapers and legos. We felt a night out would be a real pick-me-up. So we secured a location, Carmon's home, invited a guest speaker, and mailed out a flyer announcing our intentions. The women were to bring a mug and $2. We'd offer hot drinks and muffins and a program designed to help them relax and grow. Mug and Muffin was about to commence!

Nineteen of our friends showed up for the first meeting. We gave away a few door prizes, listened to the guest speaker, and sipped hot drinks. A lively discussion followed. We decided to meet monthly with a different mom hosting each time and two or three others providing the muffins.

Our little meeting has since grown into a monthly group with over 120 moms on the mailing list. Some nights are lighthearted with speakers addressing such topics such as home organization, wardrobe planning, or decorating. We also tackle more serious issues such as contentment, marriage, or parenting. Sometimes we have a panel discussion or just a brainstorming night.

Though different women attend each month, one thing is consistent each time we meet. The hostess who greets the moms at the door is met with deep, relaxed sighs of relief and warm smiles as they look forward to a night to unwind and take in some adult conversation.

ONLINE COMMUNITY

If you are too busy to commit to a group, live in a rural setting, serve on the mission field, or live overseas and want to connect with a group of mothers on a regular basis, an Internet community may work well for you. Our Hearts at Home website (www.hearts-at-home.org) offers a very active bulletin board where a community of closely connected mothers has formed. This community of women posts questions and answers about pertinent parenting challenges and also offers an online book discussion each month.

DARLA'S STORY

My husband and I both desired a small group of friends we could get to know. We also wanted the group to provide an opportunity for learning and growing in our faith as well as in marriage and parenting skills. We asked three couples from our church to join us for a small group that would meet every Friday night.

We decided to make it a unique small group experience for both the men and the women by rotating an eight-week study schedule. For eight weeks the men visit and watch the kids upstairs while the moms meet to discuss a book or topic downstairs. Then for the next eight weeks we trade places, and the moms watch the kids upstairs while the dads meet downstairs and discuss a book or topic of their choice. We usually meet in our separate groups for an hour and then enjoy a second hour of visiting as couples. This arrangement allows for relationship building as well as accountability and study opportunities. The built-in babysitting makes it a win-win situation for all involved.

START-UP CONSIDERATIONS

How do you start a small moms group? Identify what you want the group to look like. Will you study a book together? Will you use a book of the Bible as your curriculum? Will you pick a topic and ask each mom to come with one idea on the topic and one question about the topic? Will you focus less on learning together and just go out for pie and coffee once a month, enjoying the natural ebb and flow of discussion? Will you meet once a week, once every other week, or once a month?

Ask God to show you the right women to invite into the group. Look within your church family or community. Women who are in the same season of mothering usually have a natural connection with one another. For an effective small group experience, we recommend no fewer than 4 members and no more than 10 to 12. The group I belonged to, led by Julie, comprised eight moms from three different churches, whose children were all school age. We met for two hours in the afternoon every other week while the kids were in school. Years earlier I was in a group of six moms of preschoolers. We all went to the same church; we met every other week, always in the evening when dads were more available to watch the kids.

PROGRAM CONSIDERATIONS

Small groups can be loosely organized (such as pie and coffee gatherings) or offer more structure and strategy (such as book discussion or prayer). The following types of programs are especially suited for small groups with a structured discussion format. See chapter 8 for additional program, special-event, and craft ideas as well as a few pointers about critical elements of a small or large group—faith and food.

TOPICAL DISCUSSION

Some groups choose to address a predetermined topic each week. There is no "expert" giving the information. The moms learn from one another. Participants share their thoughts and experiences while a facilitator keeps the discussion on track. This option works particularly well in small groups.

Topics discussed might include: 101 Things to Do with Your Kids on a Rainy Day, Creative Date Ideas, Practical Money-saving Strategies for Living on One Income, The Power of Prayer, Organizational Tips Every Mom Needs to Know, The ABCs of a Healthy Marriage, Teaching Your Children about God on a Daily Basis, Making Memories with Traditions. These topics lend themselves to a discussion in which each mom can participate.

If you choose topical discussions as your primary programming, look for a good facilitator to keep discussions going. This person should be a mom who knows how to ask questions, draw others into the discussion, and share ideas herself to keep the momentum going. For this style of program, it is helpful to post the topics for the entire year right from the beginning. This way the moms can be thinking about the topics in advance and be ready for the discussion.

BOOK DISCUSSION

When Mom2Mom started in my home, I had just finished Elise Arndt's book, *A Mother's Touch*.[5] This book had changed my life, and I wanted my new friends to have the same experience. During our first year together, we used the book as our curriculum. We ordered enough copies of the book for each of us and then read one chapter on our own each week. I facilitated a discussion on the chapter at our weekly meeting. That particular book had a leader's guide that could be ordered separately (now unavailable), which was helpful to me as I prepared for our discussions. This is one of the reasons Hearts at Home has developed the Workshop Series books, which include leader's guides.

In a small group, you might consider sharing the responsibilities of facilitating the discussions. Each mom would be assigned one or two chapters for which she would lead the discussion. This gives each mom a sense of ownership and deepens her level of involvement. If group members are not accustomed to facilitating discussions, we especially recommend resources that include leader's guides. Each book in the Hearts at Home Workshop

Series is for the individual reader, but a leader's guide in the back gives direction to group discussion and application. Leader's guides also include relationship-building ideas (get-to-know-you-better activities), such as those found in chapter 15 of this book.

VIDEO DISCUSSION

Some moms groups have chosen to rent or purchase video curriculum. Many Christian bookstores rent videos of speakers, such as Liz Curtis Higgs, Chonda Pierce, and others whose messages are designed to encourage moms. Hearts at Home also offers videos for purchase from our conference events. Although some expense is involved, it is still an affordable option for most groups. A regional denominational lending library may have some of these resources available.

LEADERSHIP REQUIREMENTS

Usually one person can manage most of the leadership requirements of a small group, but it is important for that leader to delegate tasks and responsibilities to other group members as needed. This gives the members a sense of ownership and excitement about the group. As previously noted, if the group uses a discussion format, the role of facilitator may rotate from week to week. One member may create a roster of names, addresses, phone numbers, and email addresses for the group. Another may research attending a Hearts at Home conference together or planning a shopping getaway weekend during the holiday season. Still another may create a rotation schedule for meeting in each other's homes and providing refreshments.

GROUP GUIDELINES

Whatever type of small group you form, it is imperative that you offer relational guidelines for participants. Some women don't know how to handle friendships. Some don't understand the courtesy of a return phone call. Many don't know how to resolve conflict when it happens. As a small group leader, you need to set expectations for both verbal and written exchanges. Here are some principles to share with your group right from the start:

- This established group is the context in which you'll meet women; your own living room is where you'll make friends. It will be important that you build relationships by getting together with one another outside of our group time.
- If you are unable to attend one of our meetings, please call the leader and let her know you are ill or have a conflict.
- Practice common courtesies in our relationships with one another: a prompt return phone call, a thank-you note when appropriate, an occasional phone call just to check in with one another.

- Inevitably, at some point, there will be conflict within the group. You may unintentionally hurt someone's feelings, or someone may unintentionally hurt or offend you. If so, please follow God's guidelines for handling conflict in Matthew 18:15: "If your [sister] sins against you, go and show [her her] fault, just between the two of you." In other words, go to her and talk about it. Don't talk to someone else about it. Get the issue out on the table, ask for forgiveness, offer forgiveness, and move forward in the relationship. (See chapter 17 for a more complete discussion.)
- Confidentiality is paramount in this group. What is talked about within the group stays within the group. This builds trust and makes our group a safe place to be honest.

QUICK VIEW OF A SMALL MOMS GROUP

Type of group:	Small group
Style of group:	Usually closed
Meets:	Weekly, every other week, or monthly
Time of day:	Daytime or evening
Type of program:	Book discussion or topical discussion
Sample meeting:	7:00–7:30 Arrive at the host home and enjoy dessert together
	7:30–8:15 Open with prayer and discuss topic or book chapter
	8:15–8:40 Give everyone a few minutes to talk about what is going on in her life
	8:40–9:00 Pray for each other
Cost to moms:	None (unless moms need to purchase a book or pay for child care; each group member may also have the opportunity to provide the dessert or snack from time to time)
Cost to church:	None
Child care:	Usually arranged individually
Leadership required:	Group coordinator
Additional leadership possibilities:	Secretary, special events coordinator, schedule and refreshment coordinator

FROM MY ♥ TO YOURS

My involvement in small moms groups over the years has allowed me the opportunity to learn from the strengths of other moms. I've not only experienced friendship but also enjoyed some relationships that will last a lifetime. If a small group is the moms group you've been looking for, ask God to give you the vision for your group and show you the right women to invite to join you in the journey. You'll be glad you took the step and will be encouraged by the camaraderie you will experience.

SUGGESTED CURRICULUM AND RESOURCES FOR SMALL GROUPS

Henry Blackaby, *Experiencing God Workbook*
Stormie Omartian, *The Power of a Praying Parent*
Stormie Omartian, *The Power of a Praying Wife*
Donna Otto, *Between Women of God*
Donna Otto, *Mentors for Moms*
Martha Peace, *The Excellent Wife*
Allie Pleiter, *Becoming a Chief Home Officer*
Allie Pleiter, *Facing Every Mom's Fears*
Jill Savage, *Professionalizing Motherhood*
Jill Savage, *Is There Really Sex after Kids?*

Chapter 8

Large Moms Group

Jeralyn, the Mom2Mom leader, started the weekly moms group by describing the harried morning she had just experienced getting kids to school and arriving on time at the church fellowship hall for the moms group. She talked about lost shoes, forgotten homework, and an argument between the kids about who would sit in the front seat on the way to school. I noticed heads nodding in understanding; these moms lived the same life.

Jeralyn wrapped up her opening anecdotes and then asked us to pause for prayer to ask God for guidance and direction. After prayer Jeralyn introduced the mom who coordinated the lending library for Mom2Mom. This woman summarized the resources available in the group's library, including a vast array of books, Hearts at Home conference workshop tapes, and donated parenting magazines. She explained the self-serve checkout process and encouraged the women to take advantage of these free available resources.

Another mom took the microphone and gave us the organizational tip of the day, which addressed packing a suitcase for small children. She held up her visual aid and demonstrated putting each full outfit (shirt, pants, underwear, socks, and matching hair accessories, if applicable) in a gallon-size baggie. If packing a suitcase for three days, you would include three (or four) baggies of clothes for each child. This way the clothing would be already matched, ready to grab, and packaged in a fun way for the kids to select an outfit! I heard several *aah*s in the audience as moms quickly saw the benefits of this tip.

Jeralyn thanked this mom for her quick tip and then introduced me as the morning's speaker. I launched right into their requested topic of marriage, talking from my own experience and encouraging the moms to keep their marriage a priority in the midst of their mothering. After I addressed the women for about 45 minutes, Jeralyn dismissed the moms to their care circles, where discussions centered on questions I had provided to complement my message. Designed to help the moms commit to action, the handouts highlighted practical ways to keep marriage a priority.

After 20 minutes of discussion time, Jeralyn took the microphone again and reminded the women that next week's meeting would be a Mom2Mom craft day. She asked the women to put their chairs away to assist in the cleanup of the room. Then she closed the meeting with prayer.

The moms went to pick up their children from child-care rooms in the educational wing of the church, visiting in the hallway along the way. Some of the moms helped clean, putting away registration information, refreshments, and the lending library. It was a great morning of encouragement as well as education for these women in the profession of motherhood.

This type of mom's ministry meets the needs of many church communities. If a ministry that serves a large number of moms is the type of group you are interested in, take a look at what is necessary for such a group to succeed. What leadership is needed? When and where is the best time and place to meet? What styles of groups are possible? What about child care? These and other questions beg to be answered as we consider the opportunity to create a large and unique community of mothers.

MOPS—MOTHERS OF PRESCHOOLERS

Before we launch into the how-to's of starting a large group for moms, let me say that if you are primarily interested in encouraging mothers with children ages 5 and under, the best place to start is by contacting MOPS International (Mothers of Preschoolers), a ministry that has been leading the moms group movement for nearly 30 years. More than 3,000 MOPS groups in the United States (and more internationally) have been formed in conjunction with a local faith-based organization (church or parachurch ministry) that secures a charter from MOPS.

MOPS groups meet weekly, every other week, or monthly. They are designed for all mothers with children from birth to kindergarten, including stay-at-home and working moms, teen, single, and married moms. Groups are as small as 10 women and as large as 200.

MOPS allows each chapter to reflect its own personality when it comes to planning its meetings; however, foundational principles are consistent among all groups: community, mentoring, practical instruction, and leadership development. Each meeting features a teaching time, discussion groups, creative activities, and a comprehensive child-care program called MOPPETS. MOPS is also built on a foundation of faith. Lifestyle evangelism is an important part of the outreach component of MOPS as many women have come to know Christ through their MOPS experience.

The MOPS charter provides the group with the how-to's of starting and maintaining a successful MOPS group; it also connects the group to MOPS International, which provides local groups with ongoing resources and opportunities for encouragement, leadership training, and guidance. If mothers of preschoolers are your target audience, look into MOPS International. Call toll-free at 1–888–910–6677 or visit their website: www.mops.org (see appendix A for more detailed contact information).

WHAT IF I'M LOOKING FOR SOMETHING DIFFERENT?

If you have a vision for a large group ministry to moms and MOPS isn't quite what you have in mind, consider the following components of a successful moms group. Your group and what it offers will reflect both the needs of your moms as well as the leadership pool you have available.

MELANIE'S STORY

I started attending MOPS when my children were small and the group was meeting at a church near my home. I found the encouragement and education just what I needed for that season of my life. However, the group struggled to survive at its initial location. Eventually our home church chartered the group, and at that time I became a part of the rebirth of the MOPS group with new leadership and a new meeting place.

MOPS has taught me how to be a leader. I started out as a hospitality coordinator; then I became the craft coordinator; and eventually I stepped in as a discussion leader. Now I'm the coordinator of the entire group! For a woman who couldn't stand in front of a high school class to give a book report to now stand in front of more than 50 women and lead a MOPS meeting twice a month, God has brought me a long way. And the MOPS organization has been vital in equipping me.

FAITH

A mother's job can be overwhelming at times. The daily demand of caring for small children often brings a mom to the end of herself. Thus this is a season of life in which she may begin to understand her need for God. Because of this, a moms group is an effective outreach vehicle. Your group may be an exception, where all participants already share faith in Christ, but most moms groups provide prime opportunities for sharing God's love with women who may not have a faith background. Here are three guidelines to consider that will help make the group feel welcoming to any mom regardless of where she is spiritually:

1. Start and end meetings with prayer. This is a nonthreatening way to introduce faith into your meeting time.
2. Avoid "Christianese," that is, words that only Christians understand.
3. Always keep motherhood the topic at hand. Even when dealing with a spiritual topic, make the connection to why it makes a difference in motherhood or marriage.

The faith component will also influence the sort of "curriculum" you want to offer. Therefore, let's look at elements of and options for programming.

PROGRAM OPTIONS

SPECIAL SPEAKERS. In chapter 7 I discussed some program options appropriate for a large group as well as a small group setting: topical, book, and video discussions. Large groups will likely be more financially able to sponsor guest speakers as well.

Guest speakers are usually from the community and can provide important, relevant information to the group. A lawyer can speak on the importance of having a will; a pediatric nurse can address health issues in children; a Christian counselor can do a session on healthy family relationships; a librarian can speak on raising a reader; and the list goes on. In addition to this, there are many moms who "specialize" in some area of motherhood: organization, cooking, parenting, marriage. These moms could be called upon to present a lesson to the moms group.

Many speakers will address a moms group without charging a fee. Others will charge a nominal fee or request an honorarium. At the very least, the group should expect to pay for the speaker's round-trip mileage if the speaker has to travel more than 10 miles to the event. If you choose to use speakers for your primary programming option, a budget should be established to pay honorariums and travel expenses.

Some speakers can be lined up with only a month's notice. Others may need to be booked 6 to 12 months in advance. You should develop an information sheet about your group to send to the speaker. This sheet would describe the group (number in attendance,

KIM'S STORY

Never would I have dreamed of starting a women's ministry. Nine years ago I opened my home the first Monday night of the month to women in my neighborhood, church, and circle of friends. I served a simple dessert, coffee, and had candy at the door for women to take home as treats. I called our monthly gatherings "Sweet Monday."

Each Sweet Monday includes a fun activity and a devotion that applies to the topic of the evening. One features a clutter auction where women bring an unwrapped "treasure" from home, and we auction items off with play money. The devotion is about how cluttered our lives become and how we need Christ to unclutter our hearts.

Over 30 women attend each month, and I've learned to not even vacuum before they come. They're too busy connecting to look at the floor! Sweet Monday not only meets the needs of any woman looking for encouragement, it's also a wonderful evangelism tool to reach women for Christ.

Kim has now created three self-published curriculum books called *Sweet Monday: Women's Socials on a Shoestring*. Each book contains one year of Sweet Monday programs you can do yourself. You can start your own group by contacting Sweet Monday, Inc., 10001 Patterson Ave., Suite 204, Richmond, VA 23233; phone 804–754–7009; website www.sweetmonday.com.

moms at home, moms of young children or school-age children, etc.), explain the role of faith in the discussions (often moms groups attract unbelievers, so the speaker should not assume a Christian audience), give the time and place of the meeting (provide directions if appropriate), and explain the process for getting handouts copied, if needed. A sample of a letter to a speaker is found in appendix E.

SPECIAL THEMES AND EVENTS

SLUMBER PARTIES, MOMS' NIGHT OUT, AND GIRLFRIEND GETAWAYS. In some seasons of motherhood, a woman may particularly enjoy activities that give her a break from the responsibilities of home. At times these are mental health necessities.

A good moms group provides such opportunities for a quick reprieve. For years we had an annual slumber party for our Mom2Mom group. An occasional moms' night out at the movie theater or a restaurant is also a big hit. Many groups like to take a trip to a Hearts at Home conference for a weekend getaway. Whatever the strategy, include some fun activities in your group's schedule each year.

GIVEAWAYS AND BIRTHDAYS. It's always nice to have an opportunity to win something or to celebrate. Sometimes local businesses are willing to provide items to give away when your moms group meets. At the very least, make sure to celebrate birthdays in some way. Some groups choose to do that at the first meeting of every month; other groups keep meticulous records of birthdays, and make sure everyone is recognized at the meeting closest to her birthday.

PAMPER ME DAY. Pamper Me Day started in a conversation with a friend over a piece of pie. We both lamented how we never had time to paint our nails or do something different with our hair. One of us suggested, "Wouldn't it be fun to have some time to pamper ourselves?" Before long we knew we were on to something. Why couldn't we make this happen at one of our moms group meetings?

We called several local beauty salons and asked them if they would be interested in donating services for our Pamper Me Day. Two said yes and agreed to send several hairstylists and makeup experts for makeover demonstrations. We contacted a local massage therapist and asked about setting up complimentary chair massages. Then we asked a few cosmetic consultants if they would be interested in providing facials and manicures. It was a wonderful day for everyone! Depending on the size of your group, moms can pick one or more ways to be pampered, and the businesses get some great advertising and the opportunity to obtain new clients.

Think also in terms of demonstrations. For our group, one of the hairstylists demonstrated different ways of styling long hair, especially in braids. Moms who had little girls with long hair had the opportunity to learn new braiding techniques.

For high-interest areas, we organized giveaways. Each woman wrote her name on a piece of paper and dropped it in a jar for haircuts. Then we called names throughout the morning to give away haircuts. We also stipulated that haircuts had to be a hair makeover. In other words, the stylist was not just there to give a trim to an existing style, but rather to give a new look.

The buzz in the room certainly indicated the level of fun the women were having. It was a break from the usual schedule and a way to encourage each mom in different aspects of taking care of herself.

If you choose to organize a Pamper Me Day, you'll want to check out local ordinances for licensed beauticians cutting hair outside their salons. You could also consider asking a local beauty salon or school to sponsor a similar morning at their facility, should local ordinances prohibit such activities.

HOME BUSINESS BAZAAR. As our group grew in size, so did the representation of home businesses. After a while it became evident that we needed to manage the weekly advertising (party announcements, special sales promotions, etc.) for home businesses. We decided that any mom with a home business could post a business card on our bulletin board throughout the year. However, the only time she could openly present her business to the group at large was at our home business bazaar, which we tried to hold each November in preparation for the Christmas holiday. We also used this as a fundraiser for Mom2Mom. Each mom who had a home business could rent an exhibit table for $10. Exhibitors outside of Mom2Mom could have a table for $20 if their home business was not already being represented. We offered our usual child care for regular group attendees so that moms had the morning to shop. We also opened the bazaar to the community to increase the size of the shopping crowd.

This approach worked well and kept the group from being inundated with every home party that was being held. It also provided a great break from the regular meeting routine, was a successful fundraiser, and gave everyone an opportunity to shop without kids.

HOME IMPROVEMENT DAY. Have you ever wanted to learn how to wallpaper? Maybe you've wanted to try a painting technique like sponging or ragging. Have you considered once-a-month cooking? Perhaps you're looking for inexpensive, homemade gift ideas?

Another great way to add some fun to a group is to offer a Home Improvement Day. We had great success with this theme day at Mom2Mom. We invited six to eight different home improvement presenters to set up demonstration booths. Each mom attended five stations of her choice for a 15-minute, practical demonstration. It was a great way to learn something new!

HOLIDAY RECIPE EXCHANGE. Each year the moms bring their favorite Christmas recipe to share at the last meeting before Christmas. Complete with Christmas music, this meeting is set aside for food and fellowship. With moms bringing enough of the recipe for everyone in the group as well as the written recipe on a card (or if you are really ambitious—copied and ready for women to take home), a cookie exchange happens along with an informal time for exchanging recipes and ideas for the holidays. This works well as a day for revealing Secret Sisters too (see below).

SPRING BANQUET. At the last meeting in May, a Spring Banquet is an opportunity to celebrate the year together, thank the leadership, and cast vision for the next year. Our group has incorporated a decorating contest into the banquet by asking each care circle to decorate their own table with a creative theme. If finances allow, finger foods can be purchased or catered to give the moms a break from bringing food each week. This is also a time to say thank you to the child-care workers with a small gift and a note of appreciation.

QUICK TIPS

Our Mom2Mom group decided to dedicate one meeting a month to our care circles. Even so, on that day we wanted to offer a short, formal large group program. So we determined that Care Circle Day would be our day to ask the moms to share some quick tips with the whole gathering. Moms would sign up in advance to share an (1) inexpensive gift idea, (2) organizational tip, or (3) book review.

We devoted 5 minutes to each area, letting three different moms share in a particular morning. The remainder of the time was spent in our care circles, catching up with one another, discussing a predetermined topic, or just visiting and enjoying our time together.

DRAMA

Some moms groups enjoy using drama on occasion. Skits can be serious or humorous and can help identify issues in motherhood to which we all can relate. Hearts at Home has published two drama books for use in your church or moms group. You can order them at www.hearts-at-home.org.

SECRET SISTERS

In an effort to connect women one-on-one to encourage and pray for each other, you might organize a secret sister exchange each semester. If a mom wants to participate in the program, on the "exchange day" she fills out a secret sister form, puts it in the box, and pulls out the name of another mom, who is her "secret sister" (secret because women do not reveal whose name they have chosen). Throughout the semester, little gifts and notes are exchanged anonymously. When the semester comes to a close, the group has a designated time to reveal identities with a gift exchange.

LORENE'S STORY

Several years ago, I invited a neighborhood mom to our church's Bible study. She balked at the thought and indicated that she wasn't ready for or interested in a Bible study. This caused me to consider the need for a ministry to moms that was a step before a Bible Study. I envisioned a comfortable, welcoming environment that would meet the felt needs of a mother while introducing them to biblical principles. After a year of research (asking other churches about their moms ministries), we launched our first year of Moms Together.

Moms Together meets monthly October through May. It features 30 minutes of brunch and visiting, 10 minutes of welcome and announcements, 45 minutes of a speaker, and 30 minutes of discussion in small groups. Our children participate in our child-care program called Kids Together.

The first year we saw an attendance of about 40 women each month, but the numbers continued to grow. Nine years later we have four Moms Together groups that meet monthly. Each group has its own coordinator and leadership; however, the programs are identical. When we schedule a speaker, they commit to present their message at all four groups. Our three morning groups have an attendance of 120–140 each month, while our evening group hosts 30–50 women at each meeting. The numbers represent the lives we've had the opportunity to touch and those numbers are multiplied when you consider the families who reap the benefits of a mom who is encouraged and equipped with biblical principles.

CARE CIRCLES

If a group is larger than 10 or 12 moms, it is best to break up into smaller groups of 6 to 12 women for part of each meeting. The purpose of such groups is care and discussion. Groups can be randomly assigned, put together based on children's ages, or organized geographically by neighborhood. Sometimes strategic care circle placement helps foster friendships and connections above and beyond regular meeting times.

In a moms group, relationships deepen when we can share honestly. When we experience camaraderie and are assured that we are not the only one who experiences emotional highs and lows, we know we are not alone. Care circles provide:

- *Encouragement.* Every one of us needs personal encouragement and a place to share both the joys and the struggles of motherhood. Smaller groups give each mom a place to do this regularly.

- *A safe place for honesty.* If a mom is having a difficult time with something, she probably won't say so in a group of 25, but she may in a smaller group of 6 to 8 other moms.
- *Care.* Mothers sometimes need physical help to care for their families. For example, if a woman is put on bed rest during a pregnancy, the group moves into care-giving mode and brings meals, cleans her house, or watches her children.
- *Communication.* Nobody wants to be left out when important information is communicated. Small groups help keep the group personal and each person informed.
- *Activities.* On occasion a small group can meet outside of the regular large group meeting time. Maybe it's a Girls' Night Out at the movie theater or a trip with the kids to the zoo. Special outings deepen the bonds within the group.

When creating care circles, we set the maximum size of the circle at 10 to 12 women. But we always start groups with only 8 to 10, leaving room for at least 2 new faces in each group. This allows for growth and also prevents the need to start new groups midyear. We find it helpful to mix up the groups from year to year to provide the women with an opportunity to develop new relationships.

Care circles, or small groups, should have a leader and an assistant leader whose responsibilities include keeping attendance records, following up on first-time visitors, calling a mom who is absent, and organizing meals or other kinds of help for any mom in the circle who has a baby or is dealing with a crisis in her life. Care circle leaders also communicate information from the leadership team and facilitate discussions when needed.

A care circle leader can make or break a group. Her strongest asset is her ability to facilitate discussion in the group. When training care circle leaders, the following skills need to be taught.

LEARN TO DRAW OUT A QUIET GROUP MEMBER. Directly ask a quiet member a question to include her in the conversation. If possible, start with opinion questions before moving to personal questions.

HELP QUIET A "TALKER" WHEN NECESSARY. The dynamics in a small group can be challenging at times but not impossible to navigate. If you know that one person will monopolize the conversation, be strategic about inviting others to share their ideas or comments rather than asking an open question and waiting for someone to answer.

KEEP THE CONVERSATION FROM STRAYING. One of the biggest frustrations a small group member can experience is when the conversation deteriorates into husband bashing, complaining, or gossip. A good care circle leader will recognize when the discussion is heading in the wrong direction and bring it back to where it needs to be. A simple phrase such as, "Let's not go there. Let's bring this back on track," will usually do the job.

CHILD CARE

You can't meet the needs of mothers without addressing care for their children. Unless a moms group meets in the evening, when mothers might find their own child care, a successful group offers quality child care while moms attend the program. Because of the extensive details of a child-care program, I have devoted the next chapter to exploring caregiving options. If you are looking to start a moms group that will include child care, you won't want to miss our discussion in chapter 9.

FOOD

I have acquired more recipes through my moms group experience than anywhere else. Food is an important part of a moms group for several reasons. First, most moms don't take time for themselves when trying to get out the door to go somewhere. It's likely that they haven't eaten breakfast, so providing food at the group meeting is a way to take care of them.

Second, it is refreshing to eat something you don't have to share and eat it with people whose food you don't have to cut up. This is a chance for a mom to eat something just for her while her children are being cared for in the child-care program.

Third, sharing food is a great way to get new ideas to use in your own kitchen. Some groups have even self-published their own recipe book of favorite foods that have been brought to their moms group.

Finally, providing food for the group is an opportunity to "give something back." A sense of accomplishment and ownership comes when contributing to a community to which you belong.

Food for a moms group doesn't need to be fancy. It can be a breakfast casserole or something more like a snack. Make sure to provide plates, cups, napkins, and silverware. At the very least, a group should offer drinks. Coffee, tea, hot chocolate, fruit juice, soft drinks, ice water, and even milk are good options.

Some moms groups invite everyone to bring something to each meeting. Other groups create a schedule, either using an alphabetical list of last names or assigning one or two small groups or care circles to bring the munchies each week.

CRAFTS

Most successful moms groups include some form of craft activity in their agenda. Some groups choose to do crafts every time they meet. Others have special craft days or include a craft once a month. Regardless of how often crafts are a part of the group's activities, it is important that they be included. Why? Because of the sense of accomplishment they provide.

Busy stay-at-home mothers often feel like they aren't accomplishing anything of substance. They work nonstop, but when they look back at the end of the day, there are very few things that a mother has done that will stay done. Crafts at a moms group help a mom to say, "I did that and it stayed done! Yeah!" Even a craft-challenged mom like myself enjoys the sense of accomplishment that comes from completing a project. Some moms may want to bring their own crafts, such as a needlepoint or scrapbook project, to work on during a designated craft day. That works just fine too.

Crafts don't have to be huge projects. In fact, the simpler the better. The first week the group meets, the moms could make their own permanent name tags. In some way, the name tag could indicate how many children a mom has. This simple craft project can provide a sense of accomplishment right from the start!

NAME TAGS

Because moms groups often attract women from all over the community, name tags are helpful at every meeting. Some groups create permanent name tags as the first craft project of the year. The registration team or craft team can take responsibility for creating the style of name tags each year. Make sure you have a place to pick up and leave the name tags each week, and supply extra name tags for moms who join the group throughout the year.

REGISTRATION

A registration process is necessary for gathering personal information about both moms and their children. When moms attend the group for the first time, a registration card or sheet should be used to secure her name, husband's name (if applicable), address, phone number, email, and children's names and birth dates. This information will be added to the roster as well as passed on to her care circle leader for follow-up. Make sure there is a box to check if the mother does not want personal information printed in a group directory. If the mom is registering her children in the child-care program, a separate card should be filled out for child care. These cards will be passed on to the child-care director (or child registration coordinator) for placement in classes according to ages. You might want to create registration packets in a 6 x 9 envelope that include a brochure about the group, a registration card for the moms program, a registration card for the children's program, and a Q & A letter about child care. This packet could be sent out upon request throughout the year or handed to a mom who attends your moms group meeting for the first time.

If the group breaks for the summer and starts back up in September, you may want to consider preregistration in August for returning moms. This helps determine the child-care staff needed and allows for care circles to be assigned before the first day. A preregistration mailing could be mailed to all moms who attended last year. The mailing could be similar to the above registration packet, but would also include a letter from the director and a schedule for the fall semester to help moms make a decision about attending again. Some larger moms groups have found it necessary to limit the number of children in their child-care program due to facility or staffing limitations. A preregistration process helps secure a place for moms who desire to return to the group; it also opens up places for new moms when a member chooses not to return for some reason. See appendix D for sample registration forms.

LENDING LIBRARY

Some groups have found the value of maintaining a lending library. This allows moms to pool their resources of books, audiotapes, and CDs of workshops or radio programs, videos, etc. Moms can check out resources just as they do at the public library. Once a coordinator is in place to oversee donations to the library and overdue resources, there can even be a self-service checkout process that doesn't require her to be present at the display every week.

Many moms groups purchase the entire set of audiotapes from our annual Hearts at Home conferences for their lending library. This way the whole group is able to benefit from the conference workshops by checking out the tapes. It requires some financial resources but makes the information available to all the moms in the group.

Another group I visited had a sharing library. Rather than setting up a checkout process, a designated table was the place moms could bring their resources to share with other moms. Audiotapes, children's books, and marriage and parenting resources were all on the table for the taking. The concept was simply "Take what interests you. If you finish with it and want to bring it back, just place it on the table for someone else to take. If you take something you'd like to keep, that's fine too!" This is a simpler way to accomplish the same purpose as a lending library.

Still other groups have provided a place to share coupons, especially for diapers and formula. This encourages moms to think of others in the group and to pool their resources to help one another.

FACILITY NEEDS

A moms group that will be open to women in the community and experience growth will need a facility that can accommodate both the moms program and the child-care program. Church buildings make excellent locations for moms groups because they usually have classrooms for both adults and children. Community buildings are also possible meeting places.

SIGNAGE. Signs are a must for any group that hopes to make new moms feel welcome. Begin with a sign outside of the facility near the road, such as "Mom2Mom Meets Here!" This will help new moms to know they are at the right place. Use another outdoor sign to indicate what door to use: "Enter Here for Mom2Mom." If a registration table is not immediately inside the door, signs should indicate the path to the meeting room and registration table. The table itself should have a sign: "Welcome to Mom2Mom!" Additionally, each child-care room should have a sign on or near the door indicating the ages of the children in the room.

MEETING ROOM. A meeting room with tables and chairs is needed for the moms. Access to a kitchen is helpful in preparing and serving food and drinks. The availability of audiovisual equipment, such as a TV/VCR/DVD unit, a PowerPoint projector, video screen, and sound system, needs to be considered depending on the style of program and the size of the group.

CHILD-CARE ROOMS. For the children, rooms with smaller tables and chairs are a plus. Nursery and Sunday school classrooms already stocked with toys, cribs, and changing tables work best. At the very least, most groups divide their children into three groups: infants (nonwalking), toddlers (walking through age 2), and preschoolers (ages 3–5). If your group attracts homeschooling moms, you may offer a homeschooling room with one caregiver overseeing the grade-schoolers who bring their own work to complete or books to read while Mom attends the group.

If a group uses a church facility, it is important to have good communication between Sunday school leadership and moms group leadership. The church may request that the moms group wash toys after each meeting. They may ask the moms group to do laundry from cribs and return it before Sunday morning. At the very least, a moms group needs to be respectful of the facility it is being allowed to use. The rooms should be returned to the way they were found (or better!).

SETUP AND CLEANUP. It is helpful to have a facility coordinator who oversees setup and cleanup. She becomes the liaison between the facility and the moms group. She finds out how to handle trash (you really don't want to leave dirty diapers in the trash can for five days only to discover them first thing Sunday morning!), toys, tables, and chairs. She also learns where the vacuum is and whether the rooms need to be cleaned and vacuumed after the group meets.

Setup for the meeting often takes place the evening before (Tuesday evening for a Wednesday morning meeting). In our group, care circles rotate setup duties from week to week so everyone shares the responsibility. Some care circles use the setup night as an opportunity for a moms' night out, because Dad, Grandma, or a sitter is already lined up to watch the kids. After setting up, they head to their favorite restaurant for pie, coffee, and great conversation.

Cleanup can be a bit more challenging for moms groups. Usually children are present during cleanup, making it difficult for moms to tend to the details of putting tables and chairs away, running the vacuum, carrying out trash, or washing dishes. And some moms need to rush off to transport a preschooler or kindergartner to or from school. We have handled this in several ways over the years. Some years we had a care circle of mothers with school-age children willing to clean up each week (with no setup responsibilities during the year). These moms didn't have small children hanging on their ankles after the meeting's dismissal, and they were willing to serve the group and the other moms in this way. Other years we have identified one of the child-care rooms as an extended-care room. With care circles rotating responsibilities, the children whose moms were helping simply went to the extended-care room where one or two caregivers stayed until the moms finished cleaning up.

BULLETIN BOARD. If the facility in which you meet allows you to have a bulletin board for the group, use it for communication. Announcements, home business announcements, and general group information can be posted for all to see throughout the year. An alternative is to set up a portable bulletin board on an easel during meeting times.

FUNDRAISING AND FEES

Because it does take financial resources to run a moms group, some groups conduct one or more fundraising events during the year. This income provides finances for the general needs of the group or helps subsidize child care or participation fee scholarships for moms in need. A fundraising coordinator and team plan events such as a silent auction, home business bazaar, or bake sale to help support the group financially.

Some groups also collect a participation fee per year or per semester from each mom involved, usually $10 to $20 per semester.

NEWSLETTER, PHONE DIRECTORY, PARTICIPANT'S HANDBOOK

Written communication can be an integral part of keeping moms connected with one another. Some groups distribute an announcement sheet at each of their meetings. Others produce a three- or four-page newsletter monthly or every other month. A newsletter might include a message from the director, the program schedule for the group for the next month, kid-friendly recipes, parenting tips, special community event announcements, and information about any aspect of the group that your leadership coordinators may want to communicate.

Your group may also want to create a member handbook that communicates important information to each member regardless of when she joins the group. This communication tool clarifies information that could be forgotten or misunderstood if it is communicated only verbally. A handbook may include the following:

- welcome letter from the director
- mission statement and/or statement of faith
- leadership contact information
- meeting schedule including program topics for the year or semester
- meeting cancellation information in the case of severe weather
- child-care fees, policies
- policies, guidelines, or Christian standards by which the group operates

Additionally, most groups publish a phone directory. Some groups use a digital camera or scan a photo of the mom to include next to her address, phone number, email address, and family information. Make sure you have permission from each mom for inclusion in a printed directory.

HOSPITALITY

In chapter 2 I noted the importance of friendship for women. Friendship doesn't just happen simply because a group of people are in the same room at the same time. It happens when a person is intentional in pursuing a relationship. It happens when one mom asks another mom to join her for a sandwich when the moms group is over.

Unfortunately, relationship building doesn't come naturally for most people. The leadership and hospitality team will need to model for and teach the group how to be friendly, because a group's approach to new faces will make or break the group.

What makes a group friendly or unfriendly? What happens the minute a mom walks in the door is crucial to her perception of the group. If she walks in the door and has to figure out where to go to register on her own, that's strike one. If she has to navigate her way unassisted to the child-care room, that's strike two. And then if she goes to the room where the group meets and sits by herself while others are having conversations all around her, that's strike three, and most likely she's out. The likelihood of her returning to this group is very slim, because she has felt neither welcomed nor cared for in the most vulnerable time of her first visit. Intentional effort to make the mom feel welcome and to introduce her to others in the room is the key.

There are two parts to a friendly group: starting friendly and staying friendly.

STARTING FRIENDLY. Regardless of its size, an open moms group should have a greeter and several "takers" ready to reach out to new moms. The greeter stays at the door at all times, while the takers stand nearby, each prepared to become a personal assistant to a new mom for the morning. Let's see what should happen from the minute a new mom walks in the door of your meeting place.

- She walks in the door and is immediately met by a warm smile and a verbal welcome by the greeter. This person is one who exudes hospitality and has a true caring heart for others. She is also the one who greets all regular attendees by name and asks newcomers, "Is this your first time attending our moms group?"
- If this is a woman's first time, the greeter warmly welcomes her and says, "Let me introduce you to someone who can help show you around." She then turns to a waiting taker and introduces the two women. The taker then accompanies the mom to hang up coats, register (if needed), find the appropriate child-care rooms, and finally the meeting room.
- Upon entering the meeting room, the taker explains some of the components of the group and meeting. The two women may want to visit the food table. They then pick

up any handouts for the day. The taker may also explain where and how the lending library functions and give other information about child care and participation fees, if applicable.

- The most important part of the taker's job is to introduce this mom to others in the group. After she finds out a few things about the new mom, she can strategically introduce her to other moms who live in her same neighborhood, have children the same age, or who share some other common bond. At the very least, she can introduce her to women sitting at the same table or standing in the food line at the same time.
- An assignment to a care circle will keep the mom connected to the group long-term. The taker would get her connected to a care circle and introduce her to her care circle leader. At that point the care circle leader may even take on the role of her personal "hostess" for the remainder of the meeting.
- The taker may also follow up with this mom several days after the group meets or even invite her to lunch at McDonald's after the group finishes for the day. At the very least, her care circle leader should do the same.
- Even if the group is small, there needs to be someone who takes a personal interest in any visitor. When this mom leaves the meeting, she is ready to be a part of the game. She feels cared for and valued. She has met several new women and feels relatively comfortable about returning.

STAYING FRIENDLY. After being in a group for a while, it becomes easy to settle into comfortable conversations and friendships, completely oblivious to new faces in the room.

A good moms group should teach its members to be on the lookout for new faces. Discuss friendliness at both the leadership level and with the regular participants at least once a month, providing tools (ideas) for how to be comfortable when approaching someone new. Here are some tips for keeping your group friendly:

- Give the moms and leaders an opening phrase to use when approaching someone new. The phrase, "I don't believe I've had the opportunity to meet you," works very well. It's much better than "Are you new?" or "Is this your first time?" because it may be that someone has been coming for a while and you just haven't had the opportunity to meet her.
- Extend a firm handshake when you approach a new mom. In doing so, you give the gift of touch, which is something we all need.
- Ask questions to get to know her better. Where does she live? How many children does she have? Has she always lived in this community? How did she find out about the group? What did she do BC (Before Children)?

- After visiting with her for a while, make a conscious decision to introduce her to another mom—maybe someone with whom she has something in common. Then the process starts all over again.
- Anytime a mom is sitting by herself, this is a clue that someone needs to reach out and have a conversation with her.
- Focus more on making someone feel comfortable than on your feelings of being uncomfortable approaching her.

Practice friendliness in your group. Talk about how to approach someone new, and then take 5 minutes every few months to practice the art of conversation networking. Give the group 5 minutes and ask them to meet one person they don't know and find out a little about her. Then have them introduce their new acquaintance to someone else. Challenge participants to do that each week on their own.

EVALUATION

It is helpful to all the moms who have attended your group to evaluate the speakers and programs offered as well as child care, the lending library, registration, and other aspects of the organization. This helps leadership know where to make changes and also encourages them in areas that are working well. Evaluation can happen at the end of a semester (i.e., December or May) or at the end of the moms group year (i.e., May). A sample evaluation form can be found in appendix D.

LEADERSHIP LOGISTICS

Now that you have a picture of what a moms group could look like, let's discuss the importance of leadership. The size of the leadership team required will vary depending on group size. However, let me emphasize the word *team* here. Starting a moms ministry is not designed for the lone ranger leader. You will greatly limit the success of your group if you do not begin with a leadership team right from the beginning.

TEAM LEADER

One of the most important jobs of a moms group leader is developing her leadership team. That is why part 3 of this book is devoted to the principles of successful leadership. Over the years, I have had the opportunity to consult with dozens of moms groups who are struggling or are looking to take their group to the next level. I too often find that the concept of building a leadership community is foreign.

The director may be very visible to the moms group at large. Having said that, her primary responsibility is to lead the leadership team, which in turn manages the day-to-day operations of the moms group; the director doesn't need to have her hands on all aspects of the group.

In appendix B you will find job descriptions for members of a moms group leadership team. To supplement that, here is an overview of leadership positions typically found in a moms group:

DIRECTOR. Leads the leadership team, oversees the ministry, and usually acts as the emcee of the group meetings.

ASSISTANT DIRECTOR. Assists the director in leading meetings and overseeing the ministry. Leads meetings in absence of the leader. She is the logical "next leader" of the group, if the director position opens. She also assists the hospitality coordinator with the initial registration process at the beginning of each year.

CARE CIRCLE (OR DISCUSSION GROUP) COORDINATOR. Recruits and trains care circle leaders. Assigns women to discussion groups by neighborhood or according to ages of children. May also organize snack schedules and setup/cleanup schedules by rotating the responsibilities among the care circles.

CHILD-CARE DIRECTOR. Oversees a team of women who handle specific responsibilities within the child-care program offered at each meeting. This team oversees the recruiting, training, and encouraging of child-care staff. They also select curriculum and consistently communicate with the moms about the logistics of drop-off and pick-up of children, the general care of their children, and program policies. (More discussion of this team's responsibilities can be found in chapter 9.)

CRAFT COORDINATOR. Leads a team of women who select, organize, and teach crafts for the group.

FACILITIES COORDINATOR. Oversees setup and cleanup each week of the meeting room and child-care rooms. She also is in charge of creating and displaying signage.

FINANCIAL COORDINATOR. Oversees a team that collects child-care and activity fees, manages the budget, and pays expenses for the running of the group.

FUNDRAISING COORDINATOR. Oversees a team that coordinates efforts to raise needed operating monies for the group as well as child-care scholarship monies for moms who can't afford child care.

HOSPITALITY COORDINATOR. Oversees a team that greets the women when they arrive and works hard to make new moms feel welcome. She also oversees registration of moms and a roster of names, addresses, email addresses, and phone numbers provided for the women to get to know one another.

LENDING LIBRARY COORDINATOR. Collects donated books and tapes and organizes them for checkout.

NEWSLETTER COORDINATOR. Serves as the editor of a printed newsletter for the group. She reports upcoming events, oversees the graphic design or word processing of the publication, and has the newsletter copied and ready for distribution at the meeting.

PROGRAM COORDINATOR. Leads a team that develops the program topics for the group for the entire year. This includes selecting guest speakers, organizing discussion questions, and coordinating special events.

SELECTING LEADERSHIP

Most moms groups leaders are always on the lookout for women who would make good leaders. However, most church-based groups find at some point they are faced with incorporating leaders that are not members of their church. As the group grows, more women from the community become involved and desire to be involved in leadership.

Because of this, a group should have a plan for incorporating women from a variety of denominational backgrounds and faith experiences. Here are some considerations:

- Identify what positions can be handled by unbelievers (i.e., room mothers, greeters and takers, etc). These are often task jobs rather than leadership positions that require leading others.
- Identify what positions, such as team coordinators, need to be leaders who are believers. These are usually jobs that require leading others.
- You might want to use a volunteer leadership application for all leaders. This helps you get to know moms who desire to lead, but don't attend your church. (See appendix D for a sample volunteer application.)
- You might also want to ask all leaders (those who will be leading teams) to sign a statement of faith to make sure there are no faith issues that would cause division within the group.
- Because moms groups are often representative of a larger faith community, it is even more important that you, as the leader, disciple the leadership and build a foundation of faith and leadership principles for your leaders. This is why part 3 of this book is so important.

TEAM MEETINGS

The leadership team of an effective moms group should meet monthly to pray and plan. This keeps communication lines open, vision fresh, and relationships growing among the women leading the group. If leadership is strong and healthy, the group will be strong and healthy. More discussion of how to effectively grow the leadership team spiritually, organizationally, and relationally is found in part 3.

QUICK VIEW OF A LARGE GROUP MINISTRY—MOM2MOM

Type of group: Large, independent moms group

Style of group: Open

Meets: Weekly, biweekly, or monthly, usually September through May

Time of day: Morning or evening

Type of program: Speaker curriculum with special theme days on occasion

Sample Meeting:

9:00–9:15	Moms arrive and enjoy breakfast
9:15–9:30	Opening prayer, welcome, general information, birthdays, new baby/expecting mother or new adoption announcements
9:30–10:30	Speaker
10:30–10:55	Care circles meet to discuss questions provided by the speaker
10:55–11:00	Closing comments and closing prayer

Occasionally there is a change in the format of the meeting. A craft or special-event day could be offered occasionally.

Cost to moms: $10–$20 activity fee per semester

                      $2.50 per child (maximum $6 per family) child-care fee each session

Cost to church: No initial cost; however, use of church facility is needed for both child care and the mothers' meeting.

If the church is willing to support the program in its women's ministry budget or general church budget, it will greatly relieve financial stress on the group leadership team.

Child care: Children's program includes simple lessons for children ages 2 and older each week.

Leadership required: Director, assistant director, child-care director, craft coordinator, facilities coordinator, financial coordinator, fundraising coordinator, hospitality coordinator, lending library coordinator, newsletter coordinator, program coordinator, care circle coordinator. Some leadership roles could be shared initially.

Never has there been a greater need for moms groups. Our transient society has eroded the natural mentoring process of one generation of mothers passing on their wisdom to the next generation. Today's mothers need to be educated, encouraged, and equipped in the profession of motherhood. Leading a large group of mothers takes a lot of time and energy, but the benefits are well worth the effort. If a large, open group is the format you have always wanted, trust God to lead the way and take a step of faith. You will receive much more than you will ever give!

Chapter 9

What about the Children?

S hortly after my first child was born, I was invited to my first moms group. It was a play-group of six to eight moms who got together once a week to chat while the children played. Several years later, I asked eight moms to join me in my home once a week to encourage one another in marriage, parenting, and homemaking. Our group met for two hours every Wednesday morning, and we each chipped in several dollars to pay two college students to watch our children downstairs in the basement. Eventually that group grew in size, moved to a church facility, and had a formal child-care program that my children attended each week.

Still later, as a mother of three children, I had the opportunity to be a part of a mother's small group. This group of six moms met every other week in the evening. In this case, each mom was responsible for securing her own child care—Dad, Grandma, or a babysitter in her own home.

More recently I enjoyed the camaraderie of a small group of moms whose children were in school. Because we met in the afternoon and only during the school year, we had no need for child care at all.

Let us explore some ways to organize formal child-care programming options. Additional forms and information can be found in appendix B.

VOLUNTEER CAREGIVERS

If the group is relatively small and supported by a church, volunteer caregivers are sometimes an option. Often grandmas (and even grandpas), moms with older children, and other church members are willing to volunteer to care for children a few hours twice a month. If they see themselves as being an important part of the vision and outreach of the moms ministry, their commitment can engender excitement about being an integral part of the program.

Some groups rely on a co-op–type parental rotation as the sole caregiving resource or in addition to nonparental volunteer care. In this scenario, each mom who attends the group takes her turn in the child-care rooms several times a year.

Benefits:

Little to no financial expense.

Loving care given to children by caregivers who really want to be there.

Drawbacks:

Volunteer commitment can be sporadic.

Moms can have sick kids themselves and may not show up on a day they are scheduled to serve.

Rotating workers fail to provide stability for the children.

A lack of continuity in caregivers can make it more difficult to provide a regular curriculum or activity schedule for the children.

HIRED CAREGIVERS

Many moms groups hire their child-care workers. When there were just eight of us in our initial Mom2Mom group, we started out hiring just two sitters for our 12 children. When our group grew to more than 150 moms almost 10 years later, we hired nearly 60 workers for more than 200 children in our now formalized Kid2Kid program.

As our program grew, we also divided responsibilities between two types of caregivers: teachers and assistants. The teacher was given the responsibility of overseeing the room, keeping the schedule of activities (lesson, crafts, playground or gym time, etc.). Even in the infant rooms, where there really wasn't a schedule to keep, the teacher was in charge of the care in the room.

Each teacher was assigned an appropriate number of assistants to play with the children and oversee activities. The ratio of workers to children ranged from 1:2 in the infant rooms to 1:8 in the 4- and 5-year-old rooms.

Workers received a set amount of pay; teachers received a higher amount because they had more responsibilities. They were asked to arrive 15 minutes early to prepare the room and familiarize themselves with the lesson and stay 15 minutes after the program was over to tidy up the room (run the vacuum if necessary) and take out the trash (those diapers do stink!). Because the teachers and the workers were making less than $600 a year, the payment relationship was informal and paid in cash each week. The church would have been required to fill out a 1099 form for tax purposes for each person that the church had paid more than $600 during the year

When we began hiring outside of our church family, it became necessary to have an application process, including a written application form, personal interview (sometimes in groups for ease of the coordinator), reference check, and background check. Many churches now run background checks on anyone who works in the church nursery or children's class-rooms on Sunday mornings or for midweek programming. If your church does this, ask them for assistance in the process. Most police departments will run background checks for a minimal fee. Others offer the service for free.

When recruiting workers, be creative in your advertising. Recently I was visiting my daughter's dormitory at the Christian college she is attending. A local MOPS group had posted signs in each hallway of the girl's dorm advertising child-care positions for their twice-a-month program. If there is a college or university in your community, post a notice with the instructors who oversee early childhood education and elementary education students to find great workers who love kids. A retirement home bulletin board is also a wonderful place to find loving caregivers who may enjoy rocking a baby. Placing an ad in local church bulletins may also secure responsible teachers and assistants. Don't forget to hire both permanent and substitute caregivers. When using hired caregivers, a substitute list is a necessity to cover a position when a worker is ill or has another commitment.

With this style of care, the workers are paid by charging parents an established fee per child. Child-care fees must be affordable for a mom on one income, however. Our moms pay $2.50 per child, per meeting, with a maximum child-care fee of $6 per family. A mom who is a day-care provider herself and brings daycare children to the meeting pays $2.50 per child, per meeting (no maximum). We offer a scholarship program to cover the child-care fees of a mom who can't afford to pay. These are subsidized through donations from other moms or fundraising efforts.

Mom2Mom rarely collected enough in child-care fees to cover the workers' pay, so we usually sponsored two fundraising events a year to subsidize the cost of child care. Eventually the church also budgeted money to support the program and lessen the need for fundraising.

Benefits:

Workers are sometimes more dependable because they are paid.

Consistent teachers and assistants provide stability for the children from week to week.

Routine is established and consistently carried out each time the group meets.

Children's programming can be similar to a preschool experience for older children.

Drawbacks:

Child-care fees have to be collected and records need to be kept.

Caregivers have to be paid each time the group meets.

Fundraising may be necessary to subsidize the financial need.

College students may have a schedule change in January, which necessitates the need for additional hiring in January.

You will have to plan your meeting schedule based on the availability of child-care workers. If you hire a lot of college students, your group most likely will not be able to meet the day before Thanksgiving, over the Christmas holidays (including exam week), and during their spring break. The end of your year will also be determined by the end of the spring semester for your hired students.

CURRICULUM, PROGRAM, AND SNACKS

Each year God blessed our group with a mom who was a former elementary teacher, preschool teacher, or someone who just loved children and planning activities for them. This person served as the curriculum coordinator for the Kid2Kid program. The curriculum coordinator and her team oversaw a four-part program:

1. Story or lesson
2. Craft to go along with the lesson
3. 30-minute video (VeggieTales, Bibleman, Psalty, etc.)
4. Snack (ages two and up)

Some coordinators chose to go with a prepared Sunday school curriculum. Others chose to teach simple concepts like patience, kindness, and sharing. If possible, the lesson included a story to read and a simple craft project (picture to color, macaroni necklace to string, cotton balls to glue, etc.). A video provided entertainment or sometimes emphasized the lesson topic for the day.

The lesson plan or story was provided for each teacher at least one week in advance to allow for preparation. Before each day's session, all supplies needed for the four components were placed in the rooms with instructions for the teachers and assistants. Sometimes two or three classrooms shared the TV/VCR and video by following a preset schedule for viewing the video in one classroom and then another.

With a gym available in the wintertime and a playground in the spring and fall, we found it helpful for children ages three and older to have some large motor activity time. We scheduled this into our classroom routine and the teachers appreciated the opportunity for the kids to run off some extra energy.

At Mom2Mom we have found the most effective way to provide snacks for the children is to ask the moms to donate predetermined, boxed snack foods each semester. We usually hold our "snack shower" at the beginning of the fall and spring semesters, in September and January. Snacks are stored in a closet and distributed to rooms a half hour before the morning meetings.

Two-year-olds are always given Cheerios. The older children can have vanilla wafers or fruit snacks. Water is the only drink available, served in three-ounce paper cups. Typically the younger children have their own drinks in sippy cups or bottles that must be marked with their names.

In appendix D you'll find a Sample Child-Care Form for children under two years of age. We require a mother to provide this form, which gives feeding, napping, and toileting information, every week with the child's diaper bag.

SECURITY

Most moms are hesitant to leave their children in a new situation. We want to keep our children under our wings at all times. So when we see attention given to their security, we feel more comfortable placing them in someone else's care.

Many moms groups use a number or name ID system for picking up children. When the child is registered, the mom is given a card with a permanent ID number. The child's permanent name tag is also marked with that number. The child will not be released to anyone who cannot present the matching number. For instance, when I register my child I'm assigned the security number 35. I'm given a credit-card-sized tag with the number 35 on it. My child's name tag also has the number 35 on it. Each time I pick my child up from the classroom, I need to present my card to allow the worker to release my child. This ID number system is also helpful when a child needs his or her mother who is in a large group listening to a speaker. Even while a speaker is talking, the number can be written up on a chalkboard or dry-erase board, indicating that the mother needs to go check on her child.

An alternate for this kind of security system can be created by using permanent name tags. The mom's name tag can list the names of her children and serve as an ID tag for picking up the child in the classroom.

CHILD BEHAVIOR AND DISCIPLINE

The discipline policy for child care must be clear to both the workers and the parents. The parent and the teacher need to view themselves as partners working together to help the child be successful in the classroom.

If a child is difficult to handle in the classroom, the parent should be consulted and a strategy for discipline agreed upon. Even if a church or group approves of spanking, a child-care worker should never physically threaten a child. In a classroom setting, there are only a few acceptable forms of discipline: verbal warning, time-out, loss of a privilege, parent intervention, and dismissal from the classroom. Let's look at each of these:

- *Verbal warning.* This is when the teacher sets the standard. She states that the child cannot repeat the behavior without experiencing a consequence.
- *Time-out.* This consequence removes the child from the relationships in the classroom for a short period of time. The usual rule of thumb for the length of the time-out is one minute for every year of age.

- *Loss of a privilege.* For example, if a child throws his Cheerios, he loses his Cheerios for the day.
- *Parent intervention.* When the teacher seems to have limited success in changing the child's behavior in the classroom, the parent may need to be called in to help establish a strategy for handling the situation.
- *Dismissal from the classroom.* This is a last option for both parent and teacher, because dismissal of a child from the program usually means Mom can't attend the group anymore as well. However, dismissal needs to be considered when a child is threatening the safety of other children in the classroom or is so disruptive that the teachers cannot tend to the needs of others.

It is not unusual for children to cry when leaving their moms. With the help of assigned room mothers, we gently take a crying child into the room and get him or her interested in play. We don't let the child cling to Mom. If crying continues, we try a walk in the hallway. It is our policy to alert the mother if a child cries constantly for more than ten minutes.

Whether your child-care workers are volunteers or paid, we suggest that you have a training session that lays out your expectations. Guidelines for discipline and for handling crying or sick children should be given to workers in written form. See the Sample Child-Care Worker Training Sheet in appendix E.

ROOM MOMS

We have found it helpful to have one or two moms assigned to serve as room mom(s) for each child-care room every week. The responsibility of room moms is to stand outside the classroom (or one mom outside and one inside) and greet the moms and children, making sure each child has a name tag and number and each mom has a security card for pickup and identification. Then they help children make the transition from Mom to the caregivers in the room (i.e., help children go from Mom to teacher without traumatizing anyone!). Room moms also provide last-minute assistance to the teacher if supplies for the morning are low or missing.

Unless there is a crisis, room moms join the mothers' meeting and then later return to the assigned children's room to assist with child pick-up. The process for picking up children should be as organized as possible. Five minutes before the end of the meeting, all children should be seated in groups, having stories read to them or doing fingerplays. As the mother comes to pick up her child, the teacher or room mother should call out the child's name or bring the child to the door.

Room moms often are responsible for laundry needs of their assigned room.

SUPPLIES

Even if your group is using well-stocked classrooms, you will most likely want to keep a small box of supplies on hand in each room. These supplies may include:

- Roll of masking tape for marking anything a child might bring into a room (diaper bag, sippy cup, stuffed animal, special blanket, etc.). Tape can also serve as a temporary name tag if the permanent name tag cannot be found.
- Pencils, pens, or markers for the teacher to use with the masking tape.
- A small container of bubbles. These particularly come in handy when a child is crying after Mom drops him or her off. When the teacher blows bubbles, it provides a much needed distraction that helps the whole room settle down.
- Waterless hand sanitizer. Not all child-care rooms have access to soap and water.
- Long jump rope for preschool classes. If the class has any reason to leave the room, such as to go to an outdoor playground, a gymnasium, or bathroom, the children will stay together and walk quietly if they have a rope to hold on to while walking in the hallway.
- Roll of paper towels for unexpected spills.
- Box of tissues for tears and runny noses.
- Pad of sticky notes. Sticky notes can be used for effective communication during the meeting. Rather than having someone check on the classrooms by sticking her head in and upsetting the whole room, a teacher can write a message on a sticky note and post it on the outside of the room if she needs a parent or some additional supplies. You may have a person designated as floor supervisor who walks the halls and checks for notes throughout the morning. This helps keep distractions in the rooms to a minimum.
- Water pitcher for drinks during snack time.

CHILDREN'S REGISTRATION

As Mom2Mom grew, we found it necessary to determine maximum class sizes. This was the only way to ensure appropriate care for the children. However, it also meant that sometimes we had to tell a mom that she was welcome to attend our program, but she would have to find her own child care because there was no space available in our Kid2Kid program.

This scenario necessitated a registration and preregistration process for Mom2Mom. Registration was always opened first to moms returning from the previous year. They could register by mail or in person at the church where we met. After giving returning moms two weeks to preregister, registration was then opened to the community at large. The first month's child-care fee was required with registration. After the first month, the fee could be paid at each meeting, once a month, or for the entire semester.

A full classroom required that we maintain a waiting list. Eventually, to reserve their children's places, moms had to pay their weekly child-care fee even if they were unable to attend every week. This policy was necessary simply because the demand for the program was so great.

LEADERSHIP

Certainly the leadership of a child-care program will be key to the success of the program. Sample job descriptions can be found in appendix B. Here are some typical leadership positions for your child-care program:

Child-care director. Serves on the leadership team of the moms group. Oversees the entire child-care program and leads the team that manages the program. She also communicates pertinent information to the moms about child care.

Assistant child-care director. Assists the director as needed. She also oversees the child-care program when the child-care director is absent.

Personnel coordinator. Hires and trains teachers and assistants as well as maintaining a working substitute list.

Room mom coordinator. Recruits room mothers and trains them to effectively assist in the drop-off and pick-up process. Serves as a substitute room mom as needed.

Curriculum and snack coordinator. Leads a team that plans and distributes lessons, crafts, videos, and snacks for each classroom.

Registration coordinator. Oversees the child-worker ratio in each classroom and maintains any waiting lists if necessary. Keeps attendance of child-care rooms to monitor those ratios. She also oversees a team that makes permanent name tags for all children.

Supply and toy coordinator. Creates and restocks supply boxes for each room.

FROM MY ♥ TO YOURS

A formal child-care program is the most labor-intensive part of a moms group. However, if the moms don't feel good about the care their children receive, they won't come to the group. It is important to develop a good program through time, attention, and leadership. This is also a wonderful part of the outreach of a moms group program, as sometimes these children have had little or no faith-based instruction. The time they spend in your moms group child-care program may be the only time they learn about God and the wonderful plan he has for their lives.

Part 3

Principles for Successful Leadership

Chapter 10

Develop People, Not Programs

Jesus gave us a beautiful example of team leadership as he invited the 12 men we know as the disciples to be a part of the vision he had for evangelism. He approached each disciple, shared his vision, and asked him to consider being a part of it.

In starting and leading a moms group, we need to do the same. We need to invite other moms to be a part of our vision to encourage moms. By inviting them to use their gifts and talents to make a difference in the lives of others, you are putting them in a position to have a front seat at watching God work. This is a faith experience, not just another volunteer opportunity. Don't be afraid to ask them to step up to the plate of responsibility. It will be a character-building opportunity for them.

My friend Doris became involved in Hearts at Home leadership after working in the merchandise area at a conference. When she offered more of her time, I asked her to come to the office once a week to assist with entering data and registrations into the computer. Eventually she offered to do even more. I could tell Doris had "leader" written all over her and was capable of doing more than data entry.

Because prayer is such an important part of leading a Hearts at Home team, I asked Doris if she was comfortable leading a group in prayer. Her response was honest: "No, but I'm willing to learn." I asked Doris if she would be willing to lead one of our teams, promising to show her how and to mentor her in the process. Her willing heart and teachable spirit opened the door to a season of growth, both spiritual and personal, as she took on a new level of leadership responsibility within Hearts at Home.

Although I was not extremely experienced in leadership at that time, I had learned some important things about God, people, and leadership. Now I needed to pass on those few lessons to Doris. I needed to help equip her to do her job with a job description and vision for the task at hand, but, more important, I wanted to help her be all she could be in her relationships. My job as a leader now took on the role of teacher. Whether you have 2 or 20 women on your leadership team, you need to equip your team with leadership tools that allow them to do their jobs well. Don't just expect them to lead, *equip* them to lead.

YOU ARE A TEACHER

Every leader needs to recognize her role as a teacher. Please don't let this overwhelm you. You don't have to have all the answers; you simply have to pass on to those you are leading what God teaches you. Moms groups need women in charge who see the possibilities in others and help them become all they can be.

There are many tasks to accomplish when leading a group: programs to plan, communication to develop, calendars to keep, details to accomplish. However, a group will greatly limit itself if it focuses only on what needs to be done. The focus of leadership needs to be on developing people rather than programs. When we develop people, we are in the position to create, organize, and manage the programs we envision.

BE A STUDENT YOURSELF

Before we can teach others, we have to be students ourselves. Are you personally pursuing godliness? Do you strive to apply God's Word to your life? Have you failed and experienced God's forgiveness? If so, you can share how God has worked in your life and spur your leaders on to experience God in their lives as well.

Do you want to be the best leader you can be? Have you ever read a book on leadership or attended a leadership conference? Have you ever asked another leader to help you hone your skills? Have you ever studied the life of Christ to follow his example of leadership? If not, commit yourself to be a student of leadership. Learn about leadership strategies and how to overcome leadership challenges. Pursue opportunities to learn more about leadership. And as you do so, pass on what you learn to those who are following you.

How are your interpersonal relationship skills? Do you handle conflict in a godly way? Are you a loyal friend who can keep a confidence? Are your feelings hurt easily? Are you insensitive to others and sometimes hurt their feelings? How are your communication skills? Commit to evaluating yourself or ask others to give you honest feedback about these skills. Determine to improve in areas where you are weak. And as you learn more about healthy relationships, encourage your leaders to do the same.

Once you have these goals in place for yourself, you are ready to educate your leadership. You will need to focus on three primary areas: teaching them to be godly, to be leaders, and to be relational. Let's take a quick look at each one of these areas.

TEACH THEM TO BE GODLY

When I started leading Mom2Mom, I introduced a phrase that was the foundation of our leadership development: "Who you are becoming is much more important than what you are doing." This is now a foundational principle of Hearts at Home as well. The bottom line is that God is much more interested in our character than our accomplishments.

Throughout the Bible, we consistently see that God is far more concerned with the condition of our hearts than anything else. When we read the "love chapter," 1 Corinthians 13, we find that the apostle Paul talks about some of the wonderful things we can accomplish in our lives: possess knowledge and wisdom, speak in different languages, give to the poor, and even give up our lives for something we believe in. Although all of these things are indeed honorable, they mean nothing if we do not operate out of love.

How do I transfer this teaching to leading a moms group? By setting godliness as a goal, I am encouraging my leadership team to learn more about God and his Word. When I focus on the spiritual growth of my leaders, I introduce God's truth to them. As they become more comfortable in their relationship with God and open their hearts and minds to his truths, he will equip them to be the leaders they need to be. This puts God in the driver's seat; and with God in control of their lives, they will exhibit godly characteristics that will be passed on to those they are leading. Over time the fabric of the entire group will be influenced by the character of its leaders.

TEACH THEM TO BE LEADERS

Most leaders become leaders because they have some leadership ability. They have a personality that people want to follow, or they have ideas they want to put in place, or they simply step up to fill a need. Regardless, they say yes to the responsibility.

But just saying yes doesn't assure them of real leadership ability. They may have a vision, but they don't know how to motivate people to follow. They may have ideas, but they don't know how to bring their ideas to fruition. They may have organizational skills, but they don't know how to invite others to be a part of the plan.

I address this more in chapter 14, where we'll look at leadership resources. For now, we simply need to understand that part of our job as leaders is to teach team leaders how to lead. When a leader feels equipped to do the job she is asked to do, she will thrive in the responsibility and soar to new heights of leadership and ability.

TEACH THEM TO BE RELATIONAL

It sure would make life easier if we all understood how to have healthy relationships. But, in reality, leadership often requires the ability to deal with different personality types and unhealthy relational patterns. Bottom line: Just because a leader is an adult doesn't mean she will handle relationships in a healthy way. Many adults still handle relationships and communication as they did in grade school: spreading gossip, harboring hurt feelings, withholding communication out of a fear of being rejected, running away from conflict—the list goes on and on. A leader who strategically addresses healthy relational skills and sets standards for the way relationships will be handled within the group is on her way to creating a safe environment in which leaders can develop their people skills.

We will specifically look at developing healthy relational skills and handling conflict biblically in chapter 17. It's important to understand that these are concepts we need to teach and talk about before gossip happens or conflict arises.

LEADERSHIP TURNOVER

My friend Doris is one of the best Hearts at Home leaders we've had in our organization. Several years ago her husband took a new job, and she had to relocate across the country, thus leaving her position at Hearts at Home. Doris and I both grieved the loss. I was not only losing an incredible leader, but I was losing one of my best friends. Doris communicated that she was leaving the closest, healthiest relationships she had ever experienced. In a letter she wrote me before she moved, she expressed how much she had learned over the years and how, if the move hadn't taken place, she could see herself staying in Hearts at Home leadership until she was old and gray.

You may be surprised to learn that Doris is nearly 10 years older than me. Yet as her leader in ministry, I still had experiences to share with her and encouragement to give. Age wasn't an issue. And as our relationship grew, she taught me much as well.

My experience—with Doris and other members of the Hearts at Home leadership team—indicates that if we place women with potential in a learning environment where we invest in them as people and as leaders, they will lead for many years to come. If we truly care about those we lead as people who have skills and abilities that God wants to expand, they will yearn to serve. When we develop people rather than programs, the programs will be accomplished and the people will remain in leadership over the long haul.

FROM MY ❤ TO YOURS

Over the years I have watched many leaders who do not have a natural penchant for teaching learn how to pass along to others what they are learning or have learned. They grasp the importance of equipping others and recognize the value of passing along learned wisdom. This is really the essence of teaching, and it is something that will unquestionably take you to the next level of leadership.

Chapter 11

Pray More Than You Plan

When we work, we work. When we pray, God works. This little saying is posted on my refrigerator as a daily reminder that I am wasting my time when I do things in my own strength—when I am in the driver's seat. If I pray and ask for God's strength and direction, I am moving over and letting God drive, and he always knows the way better than I do.

Just as God knows what is best for your life, he also knows what is best for your moms group. He knows the needs of the moms even better than you do. He knows the answers to all the decisions that need to be made. He is wise and will give direction when asked. He is all-knowing (omniscient), all-powerful (omnipotent), and always present (omnipresent). God cares more than we can imagine about even the smallest details of leadership. He is never-changing, a rock, our firm foundation. If God is truly all of these things, why do we try to do ministry without him?

Most ministries and even many churches make prayer simply a formality. It's a convenient way to call meetings to order and to open and close gatherings of people. It's not that we don't have a reverence for God—we do. However, the practice does come from a basic belief in approaching God as a rubber stamp for the decisions we make rather than approaching him truly seeking his direction and wisdom. There is a difference between praying, "Here we are, God; please bless us," and "Lord, we really don't presume to know what to do and how to run this ministry. Please show us your direction and your plans. Help us to listen for your voice. Keep us expectant of hearing you speak. Show us the way."

To be an effective leadership team, we have to be a people of prayer. All ministry must be built on prayer and continue in prayer. We know, however, that prayer doesn't come naturally for everyone. For many, praying individually or corporately is a big step out of the comfort zone. But it is an important step to take. Not only will it take your team to a new level, it will take your personal prayer life to an exciting place!

All Hearts at Home leadership team and planning team meetings begin with prayer—not just an opening prayer, but conversational prayer with all women present; not just for 2 minutes, but for 15 to 45 minutes. Is this a challenge for you? I know it was for me until I discovered Moms In Touch and began praying one hour a week with other mothers for my children and their school. My prayer life was also influenced by Bill Hybels' book *Too*

Busy Not to Pray.[6] What I want to share with you comes not only from my own experience but from those two resources as well.

Let me clarify that I am talking about corporate prayer in your leadership team meetings and not at open moms group meetings, which may well be made up of women from various faith backgrounds and even the unchurched. Although it is important to start and end your moms meetings in prayer and is fine to talk about prayer on occasion, you may scare away an unbeliever by expecting group prayer. Having said that, my hope is that you would allow prayer to be the foundation of everything you do in your moms group. Trust God to lead. Let him show you the way.

Let's explore three different aspects of prayer: prayer basics—why and how, our personal prayer life, and praying with others.

PRAYER BASICS: WHY AND HOW?

Prayer is important in our personal life as well as corporately with those whom we minister. Why should we pray?

1. Prayer provides conversation with God. He wants us to talk with him!
2. Prayer provides a channel for God's power. He will never force himself upon us, but he is waiting for us to ask.
3. Prayer provides a lifestyle example for your children. What you do is more important than what you say.
4. Prayer provides the key to unlocking God's power in your life! Remember, when we work, we work; when we pray, God works.

Why should we talk with God? Because he is willing, he is able, he is generous, and he loves us! Because he desires to meet with us daily to discuss our life and what is going on in it.

How should we pray? God gives us a pattern for prayer in the Bible. When teaching about prayer, Jesus said, "When you pray, pray like this . . ." and then he proceeded to speak what we now know as the Lord's Prayer. When you read the Lord's Prayer in its biblical context, you see that Jesus was giving us a template for prayer, not necessarily a prayer to be recited. His "pray like this" template includes four specific areas.

First we see *praise* in the words "hallowed be thy name." That phrase means simply "God, you are holy." Jesus' prayer also includes the words "forgive us our trespasses as we forgive those who trespass against us." In this phrase Jesus shows us the importance of *confession,* and *repentance* (asking for forgiveness). Finally, we see the importance of *lifting up our needs* to him. We see this in the phrases "Give us this day our daily bread" and "Lead us not into temptation, but deliver us from evil." And the Lord's Prayer begins and ends with a yielding to God's will: "Thy kingdom come; thy will be done . . . for thine is the kingdom and the power and the glory forever."

You might remember this pattern with the acronym PRAY:

Praise
Repent
Ask
Yield

Other New Testament verses instruct us to *thank* God; for example, "Give thanks in all circumstances, for this is God's will for you in Christ Jesus" (1 Thess. 5:18). Another common and helpful pattern for our conversation with God is also easily remembered by an acronym—ACTS:

Adoration (praising God for his attributes)
Confession (naming our sins and asking for forgiveness)
Thanksgiving (expressing thanks for what God has done and is doing)
Supplication (asking God to supply our needs and the needs of others)
Silence (I like to add this second *S* to remind myself to give God time to talk.)

I recommend having a pattern to your prayer. You may even come up with your own. Just remember to come before God with more than a "shopping list" of "wants."

Let's walk through the ACTS pattern for communicating with God both privately and corporately.

ADORATION

During a prayer time, it is important to begin with adoration and praise. This is hard for some of us to do. We are used to thanking God for things, we're pretty good at asking him for things (supplication), and we can even confess things without too much trouble, but to talk to God about who he is and to praise him for that is something we don't do very often.

Adoration—Why?

1. It sets the tone of the entire prayer.
2. It reminds us of God's identity.
3. It purifies the one who is praying.
4. God is worthy of adoration.

Adoration—How?

1. Focus on his attributes (see list below).

2. Pick out a psalm of praise and read it to him (e.g., Psalms 8, 19, 23, 46, 95, 100, 148).
3. Sing to God a song of praise!
4. Become comfortable saying, "God, I praise you for your _____," or "Lord, you are worthy of praise because you are _____."

Here are some attributes and names of God to help you get started:

Able	Jehovah
Almighty	Judge
Beautiful	Just
Benevolent	Kind
Comforter	King
Compassionate	Lamb
Counselor	Life
Deliverer	Light
Everlasting Life	Lord
Faithful	Lord Most High
Father	Lord of Heaven
Forgiver	Love
Fortress	Majesty
Glorious	Marvelous
Good	Mediator
Great	Merciful
Healer	Mighty God
Helper	Near
Holy	Omnipotent
Hope	Omnipresent
Immutable	Omniscient
Intercessor	Prince of Peace

Provider	Trustworthy
Rock	Unchanging
Savior	Unfailing
Shepherd	Victorious
Shield	Wise
Sovereign	Wonderful
Strength	Word
True	Worthy of Praise

CONFESSION

Our times of prayer also should include confession. In a group setting this can be done silently or aloud. It is usually best if it follows a time of adoration; we have been reminded of who God is, and now we need to be reminded of who we are and of our need for his forgiveness. Coming before God so humbly, we are then ready to thank him and ask for our specific needs.

Confession—Why?

1. Your conscience will be cleaned.
2. You will feel the relief of forgiveness.
3. When we are totally honest about our sins, we begin to desire change in our lives.

Confession—How?

1. Be specific.
2. Call your sins by name (judgment, lying, jealousy, selfishness, coveting, stealing, etc.).
3. Claim the promise of 1 John 1:9: "If we confess our sins, he is faithful and just and will forgive us our sins and purify us from all unrighteousness."

THANKSGIVING

Thanksgiving is an important part of our prayer life. Most of us are comfortable giving thanks, but it's easy to skip over it when we're coming to God with our needs.

Thanksgiving—Why?

1. "Give thanks in all circumstances, for this is God's will for you in Christ Jesus" (1 Thess. 5:18).
2. There is a difference between feeling grateful and expressing thanks (Luke 17:11–19).

Thanksgiving—How?

Thank God for four kinds of blessings:

1. Answered prayer
2. Spiritual blessings (attitudes)
3. Relational blessings (people)
4. Material blessings (things)

SUPPLICATION

Most of us are accustomed to coming to God when we need something, so supplication is the most comfortable part of prayer for us.

Supplication—Why?

1. "You want something but don't get it. You kill and covet, but you cannot have what you want. You quarrel and fight. You do not have, because you do not ask God" (James 4:2).
2. "Do not be anxious about anything, but in everything, by prayer and petition, with thanksgiving, present your requests to God" (Phil. 4:6).

Supplication—How?

1. Pray for ministry.
2. Pray for people.
3. Pray for our families.
4. Pray for our personal needs.

Bill Hybels suggests in *Too Busy Not to Pray* that we yield our requests to God, asking ourselves questions such as, Will it bring glory to God? Will it advance his kingdom? Will it help people grow? Will it help me to grow spiritually?

He also outlines reasons why we may feel our requests are not answered: If the request is wrong, God says "no." If the timing is wrong, God says "slow." If we are wrong, God says "grow." But if the request is right, the timing is right, and we are right, God says "GO!"[7]

Hybels also mentions six "prayer busters" that get in the way of our prayers: prayerlessness, unconfessed sins, unresolved relational conflict (see Matt. 5:23–24), selfishness, uncaring attitude, and inadequate faith.[8] (Are these areas in which God wants you to "grow"?)

Our prayer life will reflect what we believe about God. If we truly believe he can move supernaturally, we will approach him in faith. We need to think of it this way: "We must look at the Mountain Mover, not the mountain!" which is to say that we need to keep focused on God's adequacy, not our inadequacy.[9]

SILENCE

If we do all the talking in a relationship with a friend, we may well find the relationship stifling. Yet in a friendship with God, we often do all the talking without expecting God to respond or speak. As you learn to listen to God, consider these ways he uses to speak to us.

GOD SPEAKS TO US THROUGH THE BIBLE. I'll never forget the day God personally spoke to me about my marriage while I was reading the book of Matthew. I read the verse that says, "Why do you look at the speck of sawdust in your brother's eye and pay no attention to the plank in your own eye?" (7:3). I knew God was speaking to me about the criticism I had toward my husband. I also realized it was time to stop praying, "Lord, change him," and start praying, "Lord, change me."

GOD SPEAKS TO US THROUGH PEOPLE. When we were considering adopting a nine-year-old boy from Russia, we sought God's direction. We found his confirming voice in the words of affirmation and encouragement from the godly people around us: friends, people in our small group, church leaders. We again found further confirmation in God's Word when we read Psalm 68:6: "God sets the lonely in families."

GOD SPEAKS TO US THROUGH DIRECT LEADINGS OF THE HOLY SPIRIT. Many years ago I was prompted to approach a woman right in the middle of a Sunday school lesson while we were both sitting in the back row. I kept feeling that I should go speak to her, but I fought the idea—after all, it was right in the middle of class! Finally, I couldn't fight it anymore. I got up to get a glass of water, and on the way back to my seat, I crouched down next to her and whispered, "Hi Karen, I haven't seen you for a while. How are you doing?" Her response could be likened to a dam exploding. She burst into tears, trying very hard not to call attention to herself. I quickly asked her if she would like to go talk somewhere privately. She indicated that she would. We moved to a quiet place to talk, and she told me that her husband had left her that very morning. She was not hearing a thing the Sunday school teacher was saying, as it was all she could do to hold the tears back. She desperately needed a friend to talk, cry, and pray with. That's what God was prompting me to do that morning—and I would have missed it if I hadn't trusted, or recognized, the Holy Spirit's nudge.

OUR PERSONAL PRAYER TIME

For busy mothers, the concept of having a regular, extensive prayer time seems impossible. In fact, when my children were small, I found that I needed to be creative about my prayer time. Sometimes I would snatch the first few minutes of nap time. Other days I would try to get up a little earlier. I learned to pray intentionally for my husband and children as I folded their laundry.

God wants us to spend time with him so that he can develop a friendship with us. Most moms just want to know how, so let's answer some frequently asked questions.

WHEN IS THE BEST TIME TO PRAY?

During the best part of your day! For instance, if you are not a morning person, morning is probably not your best time. Try right after lunch or in the evening before bed. Most important, make an appointment with God and keep it regularly.

WHERE SHOULD I PRAY?

Somewhere quiet!

1. Turn off the phone.
2. Keep paper and pen handy for your distracting "to-do" list that will invariably come to your head while you are trying to be quiet. Don't be afraid to stop and write something down as you pray. Having done so will allow you to return to your prayer with a more focused mind.
3. Create a "prayer place" in your home. This is a place where you keep your Bible, a devotional, pen and paper, and maybe even some note cards to write a quick note to someone you've prayed for.
4. Pray in front of your children at times. I used to find myself frustrated when my children would interrupt my prayer time until I realized that it was important for them to see Mom spending time with God.

HOW SHOULD I PRAY?

1. Use a pattern for prayer such as ACTS or PRAY.
2. Consider writing your prayers like letters. This forces you to be specific, keeps your mind from wandering, and helps you to see when God answers prayers. Use a notebook or journal to keep your prayers together.
3. Pray aloud sometimes. As we grow in our personal prayer life, we will become more comfortable hearing our own voice talking to God, and ultimately we will become more comfortable praying with others.

When it comes to our personal prayer life, the most important thing to remember is that prayer is not just a time in our day, it's a lifestyle.

PRAYING WITH OTHERS

Most of us will approach prayer in the same way we experienced it in the home where we grew up. When I was a child, one person in my family prayed before meals, so when I grew up, one person in our family prayed before meals at home. If prayer was something your childhood family did only in church, the concept of praying together aloud may be foreign. When introducing the concept of praying together to your leadership team, you may start by asking each woman to share how prayer has been a part of her life. This is a great relational growth activity and also serves as a foundation to talk about spiritual growth.

I knew little about corporate prayer until I connected with Moms In Touch. My husband had picked up some information about the ministry at a conference exhibit booth, and the concept of praying with other moms for our children and their schools was appealing to me as I was sending my first child off to kindergarten.

I called the name on the brochure and talked with a kind woman who told me that unfortunately there wasn't a group for my daughter's school. She then asked if I would be interested in starting one. I stammered that I just wasn't sure, but I would think about it. Quite honestly, I was overwhelmed with the thought. I had never prayed with a group of people, and I certainly had never prayed for more than two or three minutes in one setting. This woman said the groups pray for an hour! What in the world would you pray about for an hour?

As we were saying good-bye, she made one final offer: "If you'll gather a few moms together, I'll come show you how to pray." That was the clincher for me. She gave me a task I could do—gather a few moms together. I said I would do that, and we set up a time to get together.

That opened the door to a new world for me—a world of spending time with God, seeking his wisdom and direction for life and ministry, telling him what he means to me, coming clean with my faults, asking for forgiveness, and thanking him for the way he is working in my life. At the end of that first prayer session, I actually felt like the one hour had only been about 15 minutes! Wow! There was so much to talk with God about!

You can help your moms group leadership team experience the same thing. Even though they are doing a job for which they very likely have no training, you can put them in touch with the One who not only knows how to do the job but also knows what he wants them to learn while serving him in this leadership capacity. As they watch God work within the ministry, they will begin to trust him more in their personal lives. As they learn about the importance of bringing every detail to God and asking for his direction, they will recognize their need to do the same in their daily lives as well.

CONVERSATIONAL PRAYER

There are many ways to pray in a leadership team meeting. One of the most exciting is "conversational prayer," as if the entire group is having a conversation with God. We sometimes call it "popcorn prayer," because the prayers pop up from all over the group as one person and then another feels prompted to pray.

Here's an example of what it may be like when starting with adoration:

Sue:	"Lord, we praise you for being our Provider."
Lori:	"You have been so good to take care of all our needs and provide for us perfectly."
Sue:	"God, when we ask, we know you will answer. You are our Rock. We can depend on you and know that you will always be there for us."
Jan:	"Lord, we don't have to make an appointment with you. You are never too busy for us."
Anne:	"God, I am reminded of your wonderful Word that you have given us. I praise you for your Word and thank you for the wisdom and comfort it gives me every day."

As you can see, no one monopolizes the time; it is shared by all. As prayer time continues, prayers are often based on what has already been expressed. When people aren't praying aloud, they are agreeing silently with whoever is praying aloud. Moms In Touch calls this "praying in one accord," and it continues in this way through confession, thanksgiving, and supplication.

CORPORATE PRAYER GUIDELINES

When praying with others, it is best to have someone (probably the leader) serve as the prompter during the prayer time. The prompter moves the group from one aspect of prayer to another. There is no right or wrong way to pray corporately, but if we start out with some structure, we grow more and more comfortable with our communication with God and with others. Here are some pointers for group prayer. Frequently reviewing these guidelines for corporate prayer will help reduce the anxiety that some experience when praying in a group.

PRAY THROUGH VARIOUS ASPECTS OF PRAYER (E.G., ADORATION, CONFESSION, THANKSGIVING, SUPPLICATION), FOCUSING ON ONE AT A TIME. This helps to keep prayers from becoming shopping lists. It also helps us to expand our ability to talk with God. I suggest you review the ACTS format for prayer before each prayer session.

FOCUS ON WHAT A PERSON IS SAYING ALOUD, AND PRAY ALONG WITH HER SILENTLY. This is the essence of praying in one accord. Feel free to agree aloud. If you feel led, continue praying about the same topic the previous person prayed about. Lift up all aspects of that topic or situation before moving on.

BE COMFORTABLE WITH SILENCE. If no one is praying, just rest in the silence. Allow God to speak to you in the silence. Spend time listening. Wait for God.

TAKE YOUR EYES OFF OF YOURSELF AND OFF OF THOSE PRAYING WITH YOU. It always seems like everyone else prays so much better than we do! Place your eyes on God; concentrate on talking to him.

SPEND TIME PRAYING ABOUT YOUR PRAYER NEEDS RATHER THAN SHARING "PRAYER REQUESTS" PRIOR TO PRAYER TIME. Many times we spend too much time talking and not enough time praying.

READ GOD'S WORD REGULARLY. Learn more about him. Knowing more about him will help you to become more comfortable talking to him.

IDEAS FOR VARYING YOUR PRAYER TIME

After your group is comfortable praying together, it may be refreshing to vary the prayer time occasionally. Here are some suggestions for keeping momentum in your prayer time:

1. Feel free to vary the order of ACTS, although it's beneficial to keep adoration first to help keep your focus on who God is.
2. Begin your prayer time with a worship chorus or a favorite recording on a CD or tape to usher everyone into the presence of God.
3. Encourage your team members to sing a chorus or hymn at any time during the adoration prayer.
4. Start your prayer time with a psalm of praise (see p. 88).
5. Distribute the list of attributes of God (p. 88-89).
6. Have each person write a specific prayer need on a slip of paper and place these needs in a basket. Let each team member pick out a prayer request from the basket and pray for it during the supplication time.
7. Choose a theme for the thanksgiving and supplication parts of your prayer time (i.e., praying for your mates, children, group, or church leadership).
8. Have each person pray for the person on her right or left during the supplication time.
9. Pray through Scripture as it comes to mind. Consider using the following specific prayer needs list.

SPECIFIC MOMS GROUP PRAYER NEEDS

Pray that the leadership team would make having an intimate, love relationship with the Lord its first priority (Rev. 2:1–5).

Pray that the leaders would have ears open to God's guidance and that they would not lean on their own understanding (Prov. 3:5–6; Isa. 50:4–5).

Pray for wisdom and discernment in all decisions that need to be made for the group (Phil. 1:9–11; James 1:5–8).

Pray that there would be unity and harmony at each woman's home.

Pray that there would be unity among the leadership team.

Pray for complete protection from the attacks of the devil for all members of the team, including physical (strength, health), mental, emotional (freedom from fear, anxiety, discouragement, anger), spiritual (freedom from the deceitfulness of sin), and financial issues (John 17:11, 15–17; 2 Thess. 3:2–3).

Pray that those who attend the moms group will long to know Christ and respond to his truth in their parenting and marriage.

Pray for protection for the attendees against illness, injury, and other distracting influences from the world that may keep them from coming to a meeting (Pss. 27:1–3; 34:7).

Pray for the attendees that they will not be just hearers of the Word but doers of it (James 1:22–25).

Pray for non-Christians to come and be challenged to accept Jesus Christ (John 3:16).

FROM MY ♥ TO YOURS

I hope you can sense my excitement about the importance of prayer in your moms group ministry. I sincerely believe it is the key to unlocking God's work in your group and fully releasing your leadership team to lead in partnership with him! Don't shortchange the time spent in prayer when your leadership gathers together. Prayer isn't preparation for the work—prayer *is* the work!

RECOMMENDED READING

Bill Hybels, *Too Busy Not to Pray*
Moms In Touch Handbook
Stormie Omartian, *The Power of a Praying Parent*
Stormie Omartian, *The Power of a Praying Wife*
Frank Peretti, *Piercing the Darkness* (fiction)
Frank Peretti, *This Present Darkness* (fiction)
Becky Tirabassi, *Let Prayer Change Your Life*

Chapter 12

Communicate Clearly

As a high school student, I loved speech class. I enjoyed it so much that I entered and won several speech contests. My father, a school administrator who had started his career as an English teacher, taught me the basics of putting together a speech: Tell them what you are going to tell them, tell them, and then tell them what you told them.

His recipe never failed me. To this day my father's wisdom affects the way I communicate as a leader. I want to explore the essence of communication and all that it entails.

COMMUNICATE WHEN?

COMMUNICATE REGULARLY

The biggest challenge that moms group directors face is bringing the leadership together on a regular basis. Contrary to the workplace, where team members are under the same roof from 8:00 to 5:00 every day, moms who help plan and organize a moms group are tending to the needs of their children and family 24/7. Because of this, monthly leadership meetings are important, especially as your group grows. Preferably taking place at a time when child care can be arranged, these times of connection give you regular opportunity to address the business of leading the group and also the vision of leadership.

Keep the meeting time consistent as well. Because our leadership gathers together only once a month, we allow at least two hours for a meeting.

COMMUNICATE IN ADVANCE

I have found that setting a regular leadership meeting time each month encourages good attendance. For example, you may want to determine that your team will meet the first Tuesday or the third Thursday of every month.

This means that rather than thinking month to month, we plan one year at a time or at the very least one semester at a time. Every August I sit down and look at the calendar and plan all the leadership meetings for Hearts at Home through May of the next year. In doing so, I take into consideration school holidays and other scheduling conflicts that I can address in advance. We do this also with the calendar for the moms program itself—looking ahead to mesh our calendar with school and church calendars. Putting these dates in the hands of leaders early on allows them to put the meetings on their calendars before other activities crowd them out.

COMMUNICATE REPEATEDLY

Moms have a lot of information to keep track of, so don't fear being repetitive; trust that a reminder will be much appreciated. Dates, leadership principles, project goals, event details—these and all the other business functions of a moms group need to be communicated over and over again.

COMMUNICATE HOW?

COMMUNICATE ORALLY

AT MEETINGS. At your monthly meetings take the opportunity to cast vision, set goals, and work together to make ministry happen. Communicate details to help everyone understand the entire vision. Give a history of decisions when strategy or direction is changed in an organization. Communication is what keeps leaders and followers in the loop and helps them feel valued in the process.

AT A PLAYGROUND. Perhaps more moms group decisions have been made over chicken nuggets than anywhere else! Moms find it easy to talk in places—like a McDonald's with a playland—where their children can play and enjoy some company. While it is important to gather the leadership team together without children at least once a month, if you need to meet with one or two leaders to solve a problem or set strategy, work with their responsibilities as mothers and try to find a place where you can talk and the kids can play.

COMMUNICATE IN WRITING

The most common communication faux pas moms groups make is a lack of written communication. Some people are auditory learners—they pick up what they hear. Others are visual learners—they pick up what they see. Anything communicated verbally (with the exception of conflict resolution) should also be communicated in writing to legitimize and clarify the information. It also gives leaders and moms group members something tangible to work with in planning their schedules.

Do you have a special event coming up? Send out a postcard reminder one week in advance—you'll get much better attendance. Are you asking someone to step into a leadership position? Give her a written job description so she fully understands the responsibilities she is assuming. Are you establishing a regular meeting schedule for your team? Type up the schedule and make sure everyone has a copy.

Some groups find it helpful to prepare handbooks each year. Your leadership team may want to put together a handbook that covers leadership policies, guidelines, and pertinent information, such as a mission statement and statement of faith. (See appendix D for a worksheet to help you determine what to include in a leaders handbook.) A participants handbook can be prepared as well. (See appendix E for a sample members handbook.)

COMMUNICATE WITH TECHNOLOGY

We're moms first. We have a lot to think about besides moms group responsibilities. Thankfully, today's technology allows for creative communication that can greatly benefit busy moms.

EMAIL. We have about 150 moms (and a few dads) who keep the entire international Hearts at Home organization running. Rarely are we all in the same place at once. Because of that, we conduct a lot of business via email. Email allows moms working in their own "office" to be connected to other organization volunteers. Without leaving their home, moms can use nap time, late evening, or early morning to communicate when their schedule allows. They can share ideas and receive feedback without having to get a sitter and attend a meeting. If all the members of your leadership or your moms group have email, use it to the fullest.

Warning: Email is not to be used to address conflict. Conflict resolution needs to take place face-to-face. It is important to set that standard immediately if your group or leadership is connected by email. Here are some common email principles to communicate to your leaders:

1. Never handle any part of conflict in an email.
2. Never put anything in an email that would cause harm if forwarded to others.
3. If something might be misunderstood or addresses a sensitive issue, it's best to pick up the phone and talk with the person.
4. Don't forward bulk emails unless they relate directly to the moms group (such as a great moms story or joke that all would appreciate).
5. Be careful about sending personal, third-person, sensitive-issue prayer requests by email.

VOICE MAIL. Most families today have voice mail or an answering machine. Using this technology can save busy moms time and energy. Teach your leaders to leave full messages, including specific questions that need to be answered. This reduces time spent playing phone tag. When the person returns the call, she may get voice mail too. But if she knows the answer or can provide the requested information, a voice message may suffice.

COMMUNICATE WHAT?

COMMUNICATE FOUNDATIONALLY

I was just getting to know some of my new leaders and wanted to set a foundation for leadership development in the upcoming year. We decided to take a leadership retreat at a bed-and-breakfast on a Friday evening and Saturday morning. The agenda for Saturday night consisted of some relationship-building activities along with listening to an audiotape by Bill Hybels in which he described different types of leadership personalities and strengths. Afterward, I hoped to have each woman identify what kind of leader she was based upon his categories.

After we listened to the tape, I opened up a discussion to find out what part of the message had resonated with each woman. The room was quiet for what seemed like forever. Finally, one brave soul spoke up. "Jill, I've never thought of myself as a leader." Her comment opened up the floodgates of conversation as most of the other women breathed a sigh of relief, realizing they were not alone. These women were not just struggling to identify what kind of a leader they were. They were struggling to consider themselves leaders at all!

That's when I learned an important rule of leadership: Never assume. Communicate foundationally.

START AT THE BEGINNING. As with most things, it is best to start at the beginning. Think in terms of your prospective leaders having no leadership background. Start by laying the foundation so everyone is on equal playing ground. Then build on that foundation with information, principles, and strategies that will go the distance.

Don't worry about being repetitive or even "insulting a person's intelligence." Simply state the agenda at hand, why it is important, and how to apply it to one's life. Don't apologize for boring your team; rather, make the point exciting by giving personal examples of how this knowledge or information made a difference in your life.

Be creative in how you teach basic skills. For instance, when teaching a group how to pray together, you may begin with chapter 11 of this book. However, several months later when you visit the topic of prayer again, you may have one of your leaders whose prayer life has taken off share what God has been teaching her about prayer. Personal experience is one of the best teachers. When a new leader joins your team, meet with her individually and give her the same information the rest of the team received when you first introduced it. Don't assume she will get up to speed by being with everyone else; give her the benefit of direct information presented in an encouraging way.

WHEN LEADING A LEADERSHIP TEAM

1. Never assume your leaders know how to pray individually or in a group setting. Teach them how.
2. Never assume your leaders have good organizational skills. Teach them some.
3. Never assume your leaders know how to resolve conflict in a godly way. Teach them how.
4. Never assume your leaders consider themselves leaders just because they have stepped up to fill a position. Believe in them and cast the vision for them.

5. Never assume your leaders know how to develop people rather than just overseeing tasks. Teach them how.
6. Never assume your leaders know how to get administrative details accomplished. Teach them how to use the church copier or introduce them to the person who will make copies for them. Introduce them to the custodian if they will need to ask for assistance from him or her from time to time.
7. Never assume your leaders will follow basic church leadership principles. For instance, some churches have a strong stance on drinking alcohol. If you don't want your leadership to drink at moms group functions, make sure you spell out those guidelines. Never assume everyone will have the same personal standards you believe to be important for the group. In this case, a participant's handbook (see appendix E) may spell out these guidelines so all involved are informed of the foundations of how the group will work.
8. Never assume your leaders own a Bible and use it to guide their lives. Show them how.

WHEN LEADING A MOMS GROUP

1. Never assume someone is a believer in Jesus Christ just because she goes to church. Teach her how to accept him as her personal Savior.
2. Never assume your attendees know how to reach out to a new mom who may attend the group. Teach them how.
3. Never assume your group knows how to resolve conflict in a godly way. Teach them how.
4. Never assume that just because you have talked about something once, everyone will pick it up right away. Review often.
5. Never assume your attendees know how to build friendships. Teach them how.

In my 14 years of leading moms groups and Hearts at Home, I have never once found someone who was insulted by the foundational information that had been presented to them. On the contrary, they were appreciative of the time I took to make sure they felt comfortable in our group environment and equipped to do the job they were willing to do. Never assume people will know certain things or respond in certain ways. Make sure you give them the communication they need so they can be free to thrive in leadership.

COMMUNICATE APPRECIATION

One of the easiest ways to lose leaders is to give them important tasks and then not thank them for what they do. Everyone needs to know she is appreciated. Expressions of encouragement and gratitude should take place both verbally and in writing, as well as privately and publicly. Here are some ideas for making sure your leaders feel appreciated.

DETERMINE TO WRITE A NOTE OF ENCOURAGEMENT AND APPRECIATION AT LEAST TWICE A YEAR. Make a note to yourself on your calendar or planner to help you remember to take the time to drop a note in the mail to each leader who directly reports to you. October (early in the moms group season) and May (at the end of the year) are usually good months for written encouragement. You may want to use the correspondence diary found in appendix D to keep track of any written communication you send out.

GIVE VERBAL ENCOURAGEMENT EVERY CHANCE YOU GET. "Great job." "You are really stepping up to the task." "You really outdid yourself on that craft project." "Thank you for your hard work."

GIVE A GIFT TO SAY THANK YOU. I am always on the lookout for inexpensive "heart" gifts that I can give my Hearts at Home leaders to say "thank you" for their hard work. A bookmark, a candle, or some gift that says, "I thought of you, and you are special to me," means a lot.

HOST A THANK-YOU BREAKFAST IN YOUR HOME. This gesture says, "You're important to me." Communicate your appreciation for the hard work each leader contributes to make the group successful.

At the end of the year, it is important to recognize your leaders publicly. Ask them to stand or come forward and give the group the opportunity to thank them with their applause. A small spring plant or other gift is a nice gesture of thanks.

FROM MY ❤ TO YOURS

As leaders, you and I are responsible for getting information in the hands of all involved. This may take a bit of strategy, but in the long haul we will find that our leaders feel more involved and more valued when they receive clear communication.

Remember the maxim, "Tell them what you are going to tell them, tell them, and then tell them what you told them." It isn't possible to overcommunicate to busy moms. Use all kinds of communication devices to make sure your message is communicated both verbally and in writing. You will reduce frustration and increase satisfaction among those you lead when you communicate clearly.

Chapter 13

Cast Vision

A new mom who had been attending our group for just a few months had shared her heart with her small group (care circle) leader. Without revealing her identity and with her permission, I opened our monthly leadership team meeting by telling her story.

When she first came to Mom2Mom she was struggling with her recent transition to motherhood. Quite honestly, she didn't enjoy motherhood and was experiencing a lot of guilt about her emotions. She struggled with feelings of inadequacy and felt ill-equipped to do this job full-time. She missed her workplace relationships and was seriously considering going back to work full-time.

However, after attending Mom2Mom for several months, a new world was opening for her. She was beginning to see relationships in a new light. She was growing to understand that motherhood is an important profession. Each week she went home with fresh perspective and new ideas that helped her engage as a wife, mother, and homemaker. Although church had not been a part of her upbringing, she was now yearning to know more about this God whom many of the women spoke of as their best friend.

As I related the story, I noticed a tear streaming down the cheek of one leader. Another listened intently, a smile spreading across her face. Still others responded with a look that said, "Tell me more." Without a doubt, each leader was experiencing a sense of satisfaction. All felt reinforced, realizing the importance of their work. As I finished the story, our weary and often frustrated child-care coordinator said, "And that is why I organize child care every week—so moms like her can experience God and relationship in a special way on Wednesday mornings."

That, my friend, is the power of vision.

THIS IS WHY WE DO WHAT WE DO

Every moms group leader will come to the point where she will say to herself, "Why am I doing this?" At a moment of frustration or weariness, she will question the usefulness of what she is doing. And at some point most of us will evaluate the importance of the job we are doing and compare it to the hassle it brings to our lives. The behind-the-scenes work that most moms group leaders do will never receive an appreciative pat on the back. Sure, public thank yous will be given once or twice a year, but that alone isn't enough to keep you setting up tables and chairs every week for your group. That's where vision comes into play.

If a leader truly believes that what she is doing is not only changing moms but influencing marriages and impacting families, she is far more likely to stick with it even when someone doesn't notice all that she is doing. Appreciation is important and needs to be communicated, but vision will go the distance in keeping a volunteer motivated.

MISSION STATEMENT

When a group begins to form, a mission statement is essential in clarifying the purpose of the organization. Meet with your leaders to select a name for the group and write a mission statement that represents the goals of the group. This statement will help everyone to understand what the group is and is not.

When Hearts at Home took shape as a ministry, we developed this mission statement: "Hearts at Home is a nondenominational, professional organization for mothers at home. We desire to exalt God while educating and encouraging women in their personal and family lives."

Our initial conference events were extremely successful. As word of our events grew, so did the suggestions for change. Every once in a while we would get the question, "Why is Hearts at Home for mothers at home? All mothers need this kind of education and encouragement." It was a statement with which we could agree, and it eventually forced us to bring it to the table for discussion.

Our mission statement helped us sort through the issue and develop a response. The initial vision for Hearts at Home, as reflected in the mission statement, was an organization for mothers at home. With mothers at home as the target audience, we envisioned being able to unabashedly tell women who attend our events, read our publications, or visit our website, that the profession of motherhood is a valid career option. We wanted to be able to give them a pat on the back for making the decision to be at home. If our target audience was "all moms," we would feel uncomfortable doing so knowing that a significant portion of the audience may be working outside the home and may be offended by the message. Although Hearts at Home places no judgment on mothers who work outside the home, our goal is to encourage women who choose to stay home for a season. The mission statement helped us filter the voices of criticism and feel comfortable in what God called our organization to do. Now 10 years later, that mission statement still drives everything we do.

Do you have a sense of the mission you want to accomplish with your moms group? You may start by asking these questions:

1. Whom do we hope to encourage?
2. What words would we use to describe the group to an outsider?

3. What two to five one-word goals can we identify for the group?
4. What sentence would best describe our purpose for meeting?

Answer these questions and you will have some words and phrases to work with to develop your mission statement. You will then want to put those words and phrases into a one-to-three-sentence statement that succinctly describes your group and what you hope to accomplish. Once your leaders agree on that mission, you will want to keep it in front of your team and your group as much as possible. Here are some ways to keep it visible:

1. Have a self-standing poster printed at your local print shop and display it at your group meetings.
2. Put your mission statement on the cover of your group's phone directory.
3. Put the statement on the top of every meeting agenda you prepare for your leaders. (We'll more fully address meeting agendas in chapter 14.)
4. If your group publishes a newsletter, consistently present the mission statement on the front page.

A mission statement will also help the group stay on course over time. We can't be all things to all people, and invariably someone will want the group to be something it isn't designed to be. The mission statement will act as a filter through which the group makes decisions about new ventures. Consider these questions when making decisions about changing a group or adding something to a group:

1. Does this support our mission statement?
2. Does this contradict our mission statement?
3. If this is in line with our purpose, how does this enhance our mission?
4. Are we caving in to pressure, or is God making it evident that we need to trust him as we enter some uncharted territory and expand what this group offers?

Groups that forget why they exist begin to experience something called mission drift, which can happen when discouragement sets in. Mission drift can happen when people in the group have differing expectations of what the group will be. This can even erode relationships, and if left unchecked, it can lead to conflict or hurt feelings. It can even eventually split the group.

Leaders have to develop a mission statement and then keep it in front of their group. They do this by casting vision over and over again.

CAST AWAY!

A leader can cast vision in many different ways. The important thing is to do it—often. Every leadership meeting should start with vision casting. All it takes is two or three minutes to share a story, a letter, or an insight that illustrates the impact your program is having on one mom, on a family, or even on the community. Here are some other ideas to get you started.

1. At each meeting relate the purpose and vision of your moms group with your team.
2. Read letters, portions of letters, or positive evaluations the ministry has received that provide leaders some feedback from people whose lives have been influenced by the ministry.
3. Share the impact this ministry has had on your life and/or allow each team member to do the same thing.
4. Introduce quotes or commentaries on the importance of the role of mothering or parenting, such as the following:

If you help a mother love her life, you will help a family. And as families go, so goes society.[10]

It is a proven fact that people who are involved in professional development activities are enriched by a sense of "belonging" and stay in their profession longer.[11]

The majority of mothers have not yet identified themselves as professionals with common goals. Therefore, being a part of an organization supports and reinforces those who have chosen this career path.[12]

No one else understands the physical and emotional demands of being at home better than another mother at home. It is important to share experiences and provide a forum for those who strongly believe in the work they do.[13]

Invest in a mother, influence a family, improve a community, and impact the world![14]

Vision is not only key to keeping leaders excited and motivated, it is also an important part of recruiting new leadership. When you are looking to fill a leadership position, try hard not to think of it simply as a job that needs to be done. Instead, share with potential team members about the way this job influences moms and impacts families. Help them to envision themselves as an important part of the puzzle that comes together to equip parents to be all they can be. Give them a "kingdom" vision, helping them to see the difference they will be making in eternity. That's when you can truly say, "It's not just a job, it's an adventure!" and mean it.

Chapter 14

Build a Leadership Culture

Ilistened as a moms group director explained her frustration. She had a mixed team of leaders. She likened her child-care coordinator to an untamed horse—lots of energy but bouncing off walls. Her program coordinator was more like a snail, quiet and even unsure. She had good ideas but was fearful of pursuing them. And then there was her facility coordinator. This mom was a worker bee, pursuing the tasks at hand with energy but afraid to ask for help, which was leading to burnout as she did it all by herself.

My response was a mixture of compassion and understanding. I remember being in the same position myself after leading Mom2Mom for two years with little help. I asked her, "Have you taught your leaders how to lead?"

"What do you mean?" she asked. "They're leaders!"

"Yes, they are leaders, but they are leaders without strategy," I explained. "They don't share common leadership principles that you have established. Teach them how to lead, and they will not only be better equipped to do the job, but they'll also experience greater satisfaction in serving."

Creating a leadership environment is one of the best strategies a moms group leader can have. You are likely dealing with women from a variety of backgrounds and experience, and some have had more leadership experience than others. Some have had no formal leadership training. For any number of reasons, some leaders will eventually bow out of their leadership positions, and you will need to find replacements. As teams are formed and then shift, you will need to know what makes a good leader and then apply that knowledge.

EDUCATE YOURSELF

Currently, within the Christian community, the focus on leadership is greater than ever before. And the focus is not simply on learning the basic principles of leading an organization. It is on developing character and living with integrity as well as developing strategies and relational skills.

You and I need to study the lives of leaders who are effectively reproducing themselves. We need to be on the lookout for leaders whom people are following and learn about their strategies. We need to learn about leadership from those who have changed or are changing their communities, their cities, and even the world.

Our first stop on this educational journey is the Bible. God's Word is full of leaders we can study and learn from. The first leader to study is Jesus. Although his ways were certainly contradictory to the culture in which he lived (and the culture in which we live now), they were effective in reproducing leaders. Jesus used strategies that consistently changed lives. Without a doubt, he changed not only the communities and cities in which he lived but the world as well, even to this day.

I am awestruck at how Jesus did this not only by speaking to the masses but more often by relating to people one-on-one. He cared about people and spent time with them. As a leader, I can learn much from Jesus' example. When I am tempted to lead by simply addressing a group as a whole, without one-on-one relationships, I am reminded of Jesus' strategy of caring for individuals. Jesus cared about the heart condition of those to whom he was ministering. He taught his leaders, his disciples, by example. He showed them how to share the Good News and how to *live* it as well. He spent time with them casting vision and teaching them strategies for making the vision a reality. The disciples watched Jesus and learned to follow his lead as he spent time with Zacchaeus, the woman at the well, and so many of the other people whose lives he touched.

Today we have leaders such as Bill Hybels, John Maxwell, and Ken Blanchard who understand the intricacies of leadership. Seminars, workshops, conferences, books, and magazines on leadership are readily available to us. As a leader, commit yourself to taking in a steady diet of leadership lessons. Learn all you can about being a strategic, intentional people developer. Identify leadership principles that will make a difference in your group.

As *you* grow as a leader, pass on to others what you are learning. Equip your team with leadership knowledge and tools that will help them maximize their leadership opportunities. As you focus on leadership development, you will build a program that will last well beyond your leadership. You will also find that you are doing more than filling a position, you are investing in the foundation of the ministry.

LEADERSHIP LESSONS

TEAM MEETINGS

As introduced in chapter 10, at Hearts at Home we have developed a leadership culture that builds teams in three ways: relationally, spiritually, and organizationally. At each team meeting the leader includes information, activities, or direction for each of these areas.

RELATIONAL GROWTH. Members of your leadership team generally carry out their responsibilities from their own homes while caring for the needs of their families. This means it is especially important for you to plan activities that help team members get to know one another better and to relationally "warm up." Women work together better when they feel they know each other well. Team members who "play together" learn to trust one another and work better together. Chapter 15 gives very specific ideas for planning the relational aspect of your leadership agenda.

SPIRITUAL GROWTH. As leader, keep the foundation of God's truth and the importance of one's relationship with him at the forefront of the team's time together. Encourage the team to seek out God's truth. In meetings you might prepare a devotional, give a personal story of God's work in your life, read and discuss Scripture—or ask someone else in the group to prepare a short presentation.

Formalized topics for activities, discussions, or talks may include:

- How to Pray Corporately (present this topic at the first meeting and again halfway through the year)
- How to Study the Bible
- Using a Concordance
- How to Begin a Personal Prayer Time
- Who God Is
- Priorities
- How to Pray for Our Husbands
- How to Pray for Our Kids

ORGANIZATIONAL GROWTH. This is the part of the meeting where the leader intentionally addresses the topic of leadership. As I noted earlier, the 11 chapters in this part of the book, "Principles for Successful Leadership," can be the foundation of a year of leadership curriculum for monthly team meetings. Other, more specific programs may cover such items as organizational tips (everyone can come prepared to share one idea with the group) and how to delegate.

One important organizational skill you can model is making and keeping a meeting agenda. Most leaders make the mistake of jumping right into the "business" of the meeting, forgetting about prayer and relationship building. Appendix D includes a Sample Meeting Agenda Worksheet, which reminds leaders to start and end with prayer; cast vision; include relational, spiritual, and organizational components; give team reports; and address new business issues. The worksheet is designed to help group leaders plan meetings so that time is used wisely and strategically. By including all the worksheet components, a leader is not only attending to the business of the moms group but is also casting vision for leadership and healthy relationships.

SEMINARS AND BOOKS

Every summer for the past six years, the Hearts at Home Leadership Team has attended the Willow Creek Leadership Summit in Chicago. This three-day seminar draws together Christian leaders who creatively teach about leadership. Although the seminar targets people in church leadership, every year we find principles and strategies that are applicable to a moms ministry. For several years I just brought back tapes and videos to share with my leadership team. Then I asked the team to attend in person. The first year, each woman struggled to come up with the finances and the motivation to make it happen. But now they can't imagine missing the seminar. The event has equipped these women with vision and tools to apply to their leadership roles. It has also given us common terminology and many topics to discuss as a team trying to hone our leadership abilities.

If you or any of your leaders can attend the Leadership Summit, either in the Chicago area or at one of the many satellite sites available around the United States, you will find it very worthwhile (visit www.willowcreek.com for information). However, leadership seminars are not the only learning opportunities. Listen to an audiotape or read a book on leadership together and discuss what you learn. (See the recommended resources at the end of this chapter for additional ideas.) Whatever method you use, be sure to expose your leaders to as much good information as possible to help them feel equipped to do the job they have stepped forward to do.

LEADERSHIP DIFFERENCES

When Mark and I first married, we found ourselves in conflict quite often. Sometimes one of us had been out of line and needed to apologize. More often we needed to learn how to accept and work with our differences. When leading, one has to do the same.

Every leader's personality influences his or her leadership style. God has wired us all differently. Differences among team members can frustrate us or fascinate us. They can cause conflict or they can complement one another. As a leader, you need to be prepared to work with people whose strengths and weaknesses are different from your own.

Entire books have been written on leadership styles. Here are a few that I've learned to identify over the years:

THINKER. Thinkers analyze, overanalyze, and then analyze some more. They work strategies in their head; they problem solve in their sleep. They don't worry a lot, but they spend a lot of mental energy working through issues. Thinkers are often perceived as not having a lot of compassion or mercy.

FEELER. Feelers tend to view their world through their emotions. They express their feelings passionately. Feelers tend to worry a bit, sometimes forgetting rational and logical perspectives. They are usually considered very compassionate, caring people.

INTERNAL PROCESSOR. These people process their thoughts and feelings inside their head. They may be thinking about something for quite a while before you hear about it.

EXTERNAL PROCESSOR. People who process externally are quick to express their thoughts. They will talk about their options for weeks before making a decision. Those around them will usually witness indecisiveness during the processing period.

ENTREPRENEURIAL LEADER. Entrepreneurial leaders love start-up projects. They enjoy taking a concept and making it a reality. They know how to motivate people with vision, and their excitement about the new venture can be contagious. These leaders do well to start a project and pass it on to someone else who will manage it long term, because they will soon want to move on to another project.

MANAGING LEADER. Managing leaders want the process figured out and in place. They will oversee it, improve upon it, and tend to the details. They are paralyzed by the prospect of creating something from scratch but ready to jump on the train when it's up and running on the tracks.

Your team members need to understand how they are different from one another and learn how to value the differences. They need to learn to operate with grace and understanding when someone handles a situation differently than they would have handled it. When you build a leadership culture that educates and equips them to become the leaders God designed them to be, you give your organization a strong foundation to build on.

FROM MY ♥ *TO YOURS*

When you focus on developing the whole person rather than just accomplishing a task, you have less turnover in your leadership team. Open up educational opportunities to those you lead. Be intentional about getting good leadership information into their hands. As you do, you will see your team rise to the challenges of leadership and experience a deep level of satisfaction.

RECOMMENDED READING AND RESOURCES

Seminars
Leadership Summit (www.willowcreek.com)
Injoy Leadership Conferences (www.injoy.com)

Books
Laurie Beth Jones, *Jesus, CEO*
Bill Hybels, *Courageous Leadership*
Bill Hybels, Ken Blanchard, and Phil Hodges, *Leadership by the Book*
John Maxwell, *Developing the Leader within You*
John Maxwell, *Developing the Leaders around You*
John Maxwell, *The 21 Indispensable Qualities of a Leader*
John Maxwell, *The 21 Irrefutable Laws of Leadership*

Chapter 15

Build Communities, Not Committees

After serving in Mom2Mom leadership for six years, Sharon was leaving town because her husband was transferred to a new job site. Sharon grieved the upcoming move; she had never bonded with women as she had in our group. It wasn't because she had enjoyed the hours spent leading our hospitality team, even though she was passionate about that responsibility. It wasn't because of the relationships made and maintained through the large, weekly meetings, as rich and encouraging as they were. It was because of the relationships within the leadership team. A special sense of community had developed over the years, and that was what Sharon would miss the most.

Strong relationships within a group's leadership can result in strong relationships within the larger moms group. But such relationships won't happen unless you intentionally and strategically build community. Relationships are as important as the business of ministry, and committees need to be turned into communities.

WHAT'S THE DIFFERENCE?

When I serve on a committee at my child's school, we become a group of people working toward a common goal. It may be a fundraiser, a school musical, or some other type of school event. When the goal is accomplished—the task is finished—we part ways with a sense of accomplishment.

When leading a moms group, we also pull together a group of people working toward a common goal. However, if we simply part ways when the task is accomplished, we will have missed out on some very important relationship opportunities.

What's the difference between a committee mind-set and a community strategy? Committees serve as a task force; communities serve as a life force. Committees seek to bring about change in something tangible. Communities seek to bring about change in one another's lives. Committees require a short-term investment. Communities make an eternal investment. In essence, communities become a small group experience of prayer, encouragement, heartfelt conversation, grace, and joy.

THE SMALL GROUP EXPERIENCE

The small group movement has become increasingly popular in the Christian community. Small groups offer at least three benefits: Relationships are developed, accountability is offered, and God's Word is experienced more effectively within a small, family-like group of people.

A moms group leadership team experiences the same benefits as time and energy are devoted to intentionally pursuing and deepening relationships. We reserve portions of our "committee meetings" for caring for the whole person: spiritual life, personal life, and friendships with others in leadership. We plan relationship-building activities that are fun opportunities to get to know one another, laugh together, and deepen friendships. When we use this strategy for leadership, we are basing it on the principle that who we are becoming is more important than what we are doing.

HOW DO WE MAKE THIS HAPPEN?

When I consult with a group of leaders and share the concept of making communities out of committees, the first response is, "How will we ever have time for that?" The general feeling is that there is already so much to cover in monthly meetings, they couldn't possibly add more.

First, this isn't something else to program; it is a mind-set, a leadership principle, a strategy, a core value. If it becomes a part of the DNA of your leadership, it won't seem like "one more thing to do." Instead, you will value it because of the difference it makes in your group and in the lives of your leaders.

Second, it doesn't have to take much time. It just takes a little bit of thought on your part. Relationship-building activities can be lighthearted and fun, or they can be serious and self-revealing. You will have to plan accordingly depending on how long the team has been together and their level of trust with one another. For example, recently I asked my leadership team of six to dig out pictures of themselves as teenagers. At our next meeting, I laid all the pictures out and asked everyone to guess who was who. We laughed at the hairstyles and the awkward time that was for us. I then asked each leader to share one memory, good or bad, about that season of her life. The whole discussion took about 15 minutes. It gave us an opportunity to have fun together and helped us to get to know one another better. There was warmth and a sense of community during the rest of our meeting.

Sometimes opportunities to build community happen outside of regularly scheduled meetings. Maybe you invite the team over to your house for a play day once a month or to enjoy a moms' night out at the best dessert restaurant in town. Every so often you could rent a hotel room and have a slumber party/leadership retreat.

THE BENEFITS OF COMMUNITY

Over the years of leading the Mom2Mom and Hearts at Home ministries, I have seen many benefits to this strategy. Here are just a few:

FEWER TURNOVERS. Because the group becomes such an important part of a woman's life, her desire to stay in leadership is strong. The relational focus makes the team an essential part of her personal life that she can't imagine doing without.

HIGHER JOB SATISFACTION. When a volunteer is happy with the personal relationships within the group, she finds greater satisfaction in the task at hand.

DEEPER RELATIONSHIP WITH GOD. When a team member is in a close relationship with God and views what she is doing as ministry, she learns to lean into God and trust him in the journey. Building community is not only deepening relationships with others but also with God.

BETTER ATTENDANCE AT MEETINGS. Because women know they will benefit personally, they are more motivated to be at meetings.

LESS CONFLICT. Because the group gets to know one another and enjoys being together, there is less relational conflict and a stronger sense of trust.

RELATIONSHIP-BUILDING IDEAS

There are dozens of ways—ranging from lighthearted games to serious discussion topics—to strengthen relationships within your leadership. At first relational time may be spent sharing basic personal information (children and their ages, husband's occupation, woman's educational or professional background, length of marriage, church affiliation, length of time living in the area, hometown, hobbies, talents, reason for interest in a moms group). Here are more ideas:

I. Choose a question listed below to ask your group.
   A. What three words would most accurately describe you?
   B. What is your idea of entertainment?
   C. What is your idea of the "perfect" vacation? (Or what is the best vacation you ever had?)
   D. In a typical conversation, do you listen more or talk more? Give an example.
   E. What hobbies do you have?
   F. If you could speak with someone about any topic, what would it be?
   G. What kinds of clothes do you prefer to wear? What color(s)?
   H. Describe your home (its organization, decorations, colors, etc.).
   I. Where did you go on your honeymoon (if all are married)?
   J. How did you meet your husband (if all are married)?
II. Ask your team to bring their wedding pictures to share (if all are married).

III.   Show and tell. Ask your team members to bring one item that is special to them and tell the group about it.

IV.   Ask each woman to share her spiritual journey. (As an agenda item, this could be considered both spiritual and relational growth.) This may be done in one of two ways: Let one woman per meeting share her testimony (allowing 10–15 minutes) or ask all women to share abbreviated versions of their stories at one meeting (allowing 5 minutes each).

V.   Ask each woman to bring a favorite recipe for which she has a "family tradition" story to tell (such as a childhood memory or a story connected to her husband or children).

VI.   When a team member moves away or leaves your team for some reason, have each team member bring a 3 x 5 card with a Scripture verse or words of encouragement or affirmation (such as what positive influence the woman has had) to be placed in a recipe file box or a basket for her to take with her.

VII.   Have a team member review a book she has read recently or one that has had a powerful influence on her life.

Outside your regularly scheduled meetings, plan fun outings with your group, such as a slumber party at a hotel or a day at the beach. Think creatively. This is a great way to build memories!

In this chapter I've focused on relationship-building activities that turn committees into communities. In chapter 16 we'll take the relational aspect of a moms group a step further—what personal characteristics facilitate friendships and how we as leaders can model for all mothers in our program how to make and keep friends.

FROM MY ♥ TO YOURS

The women with whom I have served have blessed my life. I have been encouraged by them and have learned from them lessons that have improved my marriage, my parenting, my spiritual life, my homemaking skills, and more. Although as the team leader, my goal is to provide something special for them to experience, I have benefited greatly as well. As the relationships within your group move from committee to community, I hope you will have that same experience.

Chapter 16

Facilitate Friendships

One of my joys as a moms group leader has been watching friendships develop among women. Many of us do not know where to start when it comes to building successful friendships. We leaders need to learn for ourselves and then pass on the knowledge to those in our larger group.

MAKING INTRODUCTIONS

When Mom2Mom was young but growing, a lot of the participants didn't know one another. Our community is the home of State Farm Insurance, and families are often transferred in and out of town. This meant that we saw a lot of new faces each September when our group started back up. Because of this, I was very intentional about introducing women to each other.

Two moms I introduced early in the year were Susan and Stephanie. Susan was new in town, and Stephanie was a new mom. After getting them started in conversation, I excused myself and continued to visit with other moms in the large group. I noticed after a month of meetings that these two were always sitting near one another. Sometimes it seemed they arrived together. Eventually I had the opportunity to ask Susan how she was doing with her transition to a new community.

She said, "It's been incredible since I met Stephanie. We have so much in common. Several days after you introduced us, I was having a pity party for myself. I wanted some time for myself, but I didn't want to be alone. I wanted to go to a movie with a friend. After complaining to my husband for some time, I finally took a risk and invited Stephanie to go to the movie with me. I had prepared myself for rejection because I was expecting her to say no. But she said yes! We went to the movie and afterwards went out for dessert. We talked so late into the night that the restaurant manager had to ask us to leave! Thank you so much for introducing us. I haven't had a good, close friend since high school."

Susan's fear of rejection is common for many women. In fact, it almost kept her from making the initial phone call and missing out on an incredible friendship. But she stepped out of her comfort zone and took a risk that paid a big dividend.

As leaders, we can help facilitate friendships. The intentional hospitality that I talked about in chapter 8 works well in any situation in which women do not know one another.

A leader needs to know how to "work the room," interacting with the women and connecting them.

TEACHING ABOUT FRIENDSHIP

Leaders can also teach about friendship. Dee Brestin's book *The Friendships of Women*[15] is a wonderful resource for understanding women's friendships.

Consider the following material as the basis of one or more sessions—teaching or discussion—for your leaders' group or your moms program.

ELEMENTS OF FRIENDSHIP

What do friendships need to thrive? Time, gratefulness, reciprocity, grace, and forgiveness. Let's take a closer look.

TIME. When our moms program began meeting in a church facility, I reminded the women, "Mom2Mom is where you will meet other moms. Your living room is where you will develop lasting friendships." This is an important concept to get across. All too often women attend groups, expecting to make friendships that will immediately blossom. But it doesn't happen quite that quickly or easily. Friendships are formed when women make an effort to find one another and meet outside of the programmed group meeting—that is, when they give each other the gift of time, causing each other to feel loved and valued. With time, in time, and over time, we learn to laugh together, we share our hopes and fears, and we find a sense of camaraderie; in essence, we open the doors of our hearts to one another.

Time alone does not guarantee a friendship, but when you find someone you enjoy being around and the feeling is mutual, time is what will take the relationship from acquaintance to friend. When my friend Doris and I were beginning to build our friendship, she would come over once a week to assist me with Hearts at Home administrative responsibilities. Of course, we often spent more time talking than filing papers or stuffing envelopes! Eventually Doris became the type of friend I could just drop in on. I would finish up the morning car pool and be heading home when I would spontaneously decide to drop by her home for a cup of tea. If she wasn't busy or heading out the door, we would sit at her kitchen island and talk about school, home, or family.

Time is a form of attention. When we give attention to a relationship—time to listen and care for the other person's well-being—we forge strong, lasting ties.

GRATEFULNESS. We all know the power of the spoken word to either build up or tear down. Relationships thrive when people know—when they hear—that they are appreciated. When we know a friend appreciates our efforts—our time, energy, or gifts—we are spurred on to be a better friend.

Gratefulness is also expressed in simple, good manners. When a friend has gone out of her way to help you, say "thank you," and then follow up with a thank-you note. Make sure you tell your friends why they are important to you. Tell them how much they mean to you. When friendships are taken for granted, they lose their energy, but expressed appreciation and gratefulness prompt momentum.

RECIPROCITY. Friendships develop through giving and taking. If I need a friend to watch my son so I can go to a doctor appointment, I have to be willing to return the favor. In order to make a friend, I have to be a friend—a dependable friend. In every friendship, both people need to feel that the other will come through for them, to help when needed, to make a difficult task easier.

Giving time, energy, or talents to another person requires a selfless generosity, as we put aside our agenda, our to-do lists, our plans, to help a friend in need. When friends are willing to serve each other, in the words of a popular hymn, they strengthen the "ties that bind [their] hearts in Christian love." Charlotte Brontë wrote that "If we build on a sure foundation in friendship, we must love our friends for their sakes rather than for our own." We must generously give time, attention, care. But there's something wonderfully circular about our selfless giving; it is in giving that we benefit the most.

For some of us, it is more difficult to receive than to give. If we never allow ourselves to be vulnerable, if we never are willing to be helped, we are short-circuiting the kind of friendship we long for. People need other people, yet often we are afraid to ask for assistance. We hate to bother someone. But when we refuse to depend on a friend, we deny her the opportunity to serve, to encourage, to express love. She needs to do those things for the friendship to deepen. She also needs to do them to grow her character as a loving, generous woman.

And when we allow ourselves to depend on someone else, when we have faith that another person can do something for our benefit, we expand our capacity to love and trust. We need to do that to deepen the relationship. Depending on someone else will grow our character as well.

GRACE AND FORGIVENESS. Grace and forgiveness are essential elements of a deep friendship. If we're honest, most of us don't know what to do when conflict arises in a relationship. Our human nature tells us to run, to protect ourselves, to hide behind defensiveness. But God tells us that relationships are valuable and that we need to handle conflict in a healthier fashion. Conflict resolution is so important that I devote an entire chapter (17) to it.

It takes courage to go to a friend and address a problem, and it takes humility to admit we are wrong. But our relationships are worth the effort. With God's help we can find the courage, the humility, and the strength to do what we need to do to preserve an endangered friendship.

When we have caused hurt, whether it was intentional or unintentional, we have to be willing to say, "I'm sorry I hurt you. Will you please forgive me?" When we have been hurt by a friend, we need to be willing to extend forgiveness. There will even be times when we need to forgive when forgiveness isn't requested.

Grace goes hand-in-hand with forgiveness. Grace is when we allow others to be human, to make mistakes. Extending grace involves making the choice to forgive one another for our human shortcomings.

LEVELS OF RELATIONSHIPS

We need to help women understand various kinds or levels of relationships. We expect too much from others if we expect every acquaintance to develop into a heart-to-heart, life-long friendship.

In this regard, I also remind women that when someone seems to rebuff their overtures of friendship, they shouldn't immediately frame the encounter as rejection. Not every potential friend becomes a good friend. A woman you would like to get to know better may simply already have too much on her plate or have different friendship needs at this time. Keep looking—and praying—for another friend with whom you can connect.

Some relationships are and always will be *casual* friendships—people you know, probably by name, at church, school, the gym, and moms group. These are people you say hello to when attending an event. The conversation is usually cliché or casual.

Some friendships are for *convenience*. For example, you may trade babysitting with a neighbor. You may enjoy chatting across the fence or occasionally over a cup of coffee. You may get beyond casual conversation, sharing concerns, triumphs, and tragedies. However, if you move across town and no longer have the convenience factor to foster the relationship, you may find that the relationship becomes a casual friendship. You are excited to see this friend when you run into her at the store, but you are content to let the connection happen by chance.

Then there are *commitment* friendships. These relationships are the long-term friendships that survive crisis and distance and stand the test of time. These are usually relationships of vulnerability; you know each other very well. Commitment friendships are the relationships most of us long for, but they are rare. It takes time for these friendships to form as you learn to trust and depend on each other.

RISKS OF FRIENDSHIPS

When speaking on the topic of friendships, I find it necessary to address disappointment in relationships. Many of us have been hurt by friends in the past, which makes us afraid to get close to someone again. Women who have moved often may find it hard to risk the hurt of leaving friends behind. Deep friendship requires emotional vulnerability, which by definition requires risk. Nevertheless, the benefits of relationship are worth the risks. We need one another!

WHAT IF A MOM ISN'T SUCCESSFUL AT MAKING FRIENDS?

Some women need a mentor—an encourager—who can help them navigate friendship. This mentor must be willing to ask tough questions and address difficult issues at times.

It is rarely appropriate to "barge in" and give someone unsolicited advice. But on occasion—with great prayer—a mentor may feel the need to ask a woman if she can "speak into her life"; this phrase indicates that the mentor is asking permission to share honestly what she sees in the woman's life that is hindering friendship. This takes some courage on the mentor's part but can sometimes help a mom identify things she can begin to change that are keeping others from pursuing relationship.

Several years ago, a mom who was not making friends asked to meet with me. She told me that she felt the group was unfriendly and that no one was reaching out to her. She blamed others for failing to pursue relationship. The truth was that she had a personal hygiene problem, and her body odor was overpowering. I had been praying for this mom and asking God for an opportunity to share with her about her hygiene; it seemed that God was giving me that opportunity. I took a deep breath and asked her if I could share a different perspective with her. She agreed, and I told her of the difficult situation her lack of hygiene put people in. The moms desired to reach out to her, but they struggled to get past the unpleasant odor. I explained the importance of showering daily and using deodorant. I encouraged her to try to improve her personal hygiene and see what happened.

Today that mom has wonderful friendships within the group. She has found her niche and has connected with some other moms who have children of similar ages. She takes much better care of herself and has seen the benefits of doing so.

What can we do to help a woman who isn't making friends? Here are some areas of evaluation that can help her identify what may be inhibiting relationships.

TO BE A GOOD FRIEND, WE NEED TO FEEL GOOD ABOUT OURSELVES. People can't fill us up; they can't make us whole. We must find that in our relationship with God.

FRIENDSHIPS TAKE GOOD SOCIAL SKILLS. If you were not trained in good manners, good hygiene, or appropriate housekeeping knowledge, then do your homework now. Begin making changes that can open the doors to friendships.

EVALUATE YOUR CHILDREN'S BEHAVIORS. Are your children enjoyable to be around, or are they demanding, mean, and rude to others? Do they consistently interrupt your conversation with other moms? If so, work on social skills with your children as well.

EVALUATE YOUR CONVERSATIONS AND TIME WITH OTHER WOMEN. Is it self-centered? Does your conversation center mainly around you, your problems, and your children, or do you seek to find out about others? Are you a good listener when someone else talks? Do you sacrifice your time, or are you selfish with it?

EVALUATE YOUR RELATIONSHIP WITH YOUR MOTHER. Your mother is the first intimate female relationship you ever had. Your ability to relate to other women may well mirror your ability to relate to your mother.

FRIENDSHIP IS LIKE MONEY: EASIER MADE THAN KEPT. Consider your conflict resolution skills. All friendships will have conflict of some sort. Can you work through the conflict? Will you talk through it? Or will you destroy the relationship with bitterness, stuffing the problem away until you can't deal with it appropriately?

IDEAS FOR GETTING A FRIENDSHIP OFF THE GROUND

Starting a new friendship can be overwhelming for some women. Here are some suggestions for how to begin.

Ask a new or prospective friend to start a tradition together. It may be going out for pie and coffee every other Thursday night, or meeting three nights a week to walk for an hour, or participating in a playgroup together one afternoon a week. When you ask someone to join you in doing a regular activity, you are taking a first step toward friendship. You're giving the relationship opportunity to develop over time.

Consider asking someone to help you with a project. You might decorate a child's bedroom, stencil a living room, do once-a-month cooking, or even have a garage sale together. Working side by side with someone provides an ideal time to share thoughts and feelings, letting the other "into" your life. As you accomplish something together, a special bond is created. Don't be afraid to ask for help with a project or goal; a new friend will most likely be honored that you requested her help. Likewise, make sure you are available to help her with her projects.

Dump any unrealistic Martha Stewart expectations that could get in the way of extending an invitation. Invite a woman and her children over after moms group to share peanut butter and jelly sandwiches with you. She's probably going to her house to eat the same thing. PB&Js always taste better when shared with a friend! Find out who she is. Listen to her story. Send her home with a word of encouragement. Do as George MacDonald says: "Instead of a gem or a flower, cast the gift of a lovely thought into the heart of a friend."

Who knows, your invitation may be the beginning of a beautiful friendship.

FROM MY ❤ TO YOURS

I always say that God showed his sense of humor by placing me in the midst of a moms ministry. When I was in high school, I didn't have close girlfriends. I had close guy friends. I liked hanging with the guys because they didn't form cliques or backbite or gossip. Years later I found myself smack-dab in the middle of female relationships, and I experienced a sharp learning curve. But I also discovered something very important in the process: I need friends. I need other women in my life, and I need to be able to give and receive in friendship. That's the importance of understanding the fine art of friendship.

Chapter 17

Handle Conflict Biblically

Isat listening to two of my top leaders each relating with tears the hurt and frustration she believed had been caused by the other.

At one point an atmosphere of defensiveness set in. As an objective third party, I quickly identified it and helped move the conversation back to a sharing and listening mode. We used the "drive-thru order" communication strategy: As each woman spoke, I asked the other to listen and then repeat back what she had heard. This way the person who spoke felt she had been heard. Using this method also gave each woman opportunities to clarify any misunderstandings in the communication.

We eventually moved into a resolution phase of our meeting, bringing closure by asking for and offering forgiveness. It was a hard, tiring process, but one that protected relationship and brought about healing.

In the weeks, months, and years that followed, these two women became best friends, often telling others about the victory they experienced by handling conflict biblically. This is the beauty of Matthew 18.

WHAT'S THE PROBLEM?

We all are human. Because we are not perfect, we will make mistakes that will affect others. We will disappoint others. We will be convinced that we are right and that they have wronged us. Conflict will arise in relationships in any arena—at home, school, work, or play.

What most of us know about dealing with conflict comes from the way conflict was handled in the homes in which we grew up. For some that model involved healthy conflict resolution strategies. For many it did not. Some of us grew up in homes where conflict was swept under the rug: "If we don't talk about it, it will go away." Others grew up in homes where conflict was handled aggressively with a lot of anger. These unhealthy strategies only exacerbate our human-relationship problems.

In ministry we have another level of conflict: A spiritual battle is raging. The agitating enemy, Satan, doesn't want your ministry to flourish. In fact, his goal is for it not to exist at all. We must realize and teach others to realize that conflict is a ploy of Satan to break down ministry. If we begin to see one another as enemies, we spend precious time arguing and disagreeing. But if we recognize the true enemy—often the source of strife in our relationships—we are able to pursue resolution with a godly mind-set.

JESUS' METHOD OF CONFLICT RESOLUTION

Yes, we are to make every attempt to avoid conflict with good communication, appreciation, and generous doses of grace. But we also must learn how to resolve conflict when it happens. God knew it would happen, and that is why he gives us direction in Matthew 18:15–16: "If your brother sins against you, go and show him his fault, just between the two of you. If he listens to you, you have won your brother over. But if he will not listen, take one or two others along, so that 'every matter may be established by the testimony of two or three witnesses.'"

Let's look at God's direction a little closer to understand it ourselves and then teach it to others. Because I usually teach this to women, I first paraphrase the verses, replacing the word "brother" with "sister." This helps personalize the instruction for women. In looking at the first sentence, it is important to focus on the phrase "just between the two of you." Notice that Jesus didn't say, "If your sister sins against you, go and share what she did with two other girlfriends." Nor did Jesus say, "If your sister sins against you, just withdraw from the relationship, give her the cold shoulder, and put up a wall so you don't get hurt again." No, Scripture says, "If your sister sins against you, go and show her her fault, just between the two of you."

If you and I want to win spiritual battles we face as we engage in ministry, we must be willing to handle conflict *God's way*, which will most likely be different from the way we want to handle it!

HOW DO I START?

If you need to approach someone to resolve a hurt or conflict, you may want to use a phrase such as one of these:

- "I'm struggling with something, and I'm hoping you can help me sort it out. Could we set up a time to talk?"
- "I feel as if there is a wall between us. Maybe it's just my own struggles but maybe there's something else there. Could we take some time to sort it out?"
- "I've been sorting through something in my head, and now I need to bring some perspective to it. Do you have some time when we could talk?"
- "I know the situation the other day was difficult. More than anything else, I want to bring some closure to what happened. Can we set up a time to talk?"

Face-to-face interaction is very important when resolving conflict. This allows for emotions to be experienced, touch to be extended, and body language to be seen. No part of conflict resolution should ever be done in writing—no email, no letters.

Notice that Matthew 18:15 says, ". . . go and show him his fault." It doesn't say, "Write her a note (or an email!) and show her her fault." No, God knows that we'll wimp out, so he makes the instruction very clear.

What is the goal of this encounter? Resolution of the conflict. Preservation of the relationship is a secondary goal. Winning has no place in the matter. We're not out to win. Our goal is to preserve relationship, ask for and extend forgiveness, and find healing where hurt has taken place.

WHAT IF THE CONVERSATION DOESN'T GO WELL?

Jesus took care of even those details. Matthew 18:16 says, "But if he will not listen, take one or two others along, so that 'every matter may be established by the testimony of two or three witnesses.'" Remember the story at the beginning of this chapter? My two leaders had followed Matthew 18:15, but there was so much hurt that they were unsuccessful at sorting it out on their own. Their next step was to follow verse 16 by asking me to help them resolve the conflict. I entered the meeting with a heart of prayer, asking God to give me direction, wisdom, and courage to help bring resolution to the hurt. It took awhile, but in the end God was victorious and the leaders experienced healing. Not only that, but the experience actually strengthened the relationship between these two women.

EXTENDING GRACE

When we are working alongside others in ministry, we will begin to notice things that irritate us. This is where grace comes in. God gives us grace, and he asks us to extend grace to one another. Grace is allowing another to be human—to make mistakes. It is approaching relationships with a heart of love and forgiveness. If the issue at hand isn't a sin issue or a "kingdom" issue or it hasn't brought hurt to another person, then God may just be asking us to handle it in our own heart with grace.

PROACTIVE LEADERSHIP

Most leaders make the mistake of trying to teach about conflict resolution when a conflict happens. The wise leader, however, teaches about conflict resolution before a conflict happens. She helps her leadership or her group to know that conflict will most likely happen, and when it does, this is how to handle it. This sets the standard for the group and gives a foundation of information that everyone knows and understands. When conflict happens, the leader can refer to the standard that is already in place. Even if conflict resolution is a new experience for someone, she already has the information she needs to go, and grow, through it.

Here are the concise policy guidelines for conflict resolution and also for handling difficult situations that are printed in our leadership handbook.

CONFLICT WITHIN LEADERSHIP

1. When someone has hurt us or we have caused injury, we will go to the person involved immediately. Explain what happened. Ask for forgiveness. Ask how you can resolve it. It is best to use "I feel" or "I felt" statements. Tell the other person that you don't want a wall between the two of you; you feel the need to talk about the conflict. Always be sensitive to what may be going on in the other person's life that may have contributed to the problem. When we go into a difficult situation, it is always helpful to give the other person the benefit of the doubt. This helps us to be less on the defensive and more interested in making a priority of caring for one another and restoring the relationship.
2. We will not talk about another woman with anyone. That is called gossip, and it does nothing but break down relationships.
3. If you need accountability, objectivity, or help with a situation, you may go to your leader. She can provide wisdom, and she will also hold you accountable to go to the person with whom you have the conflict. She will not get in the middle.
4. Forgive the other person. Forgiveness is a choice, and we need to exercise it in our relationships. This is the key to a continued working relationship. When we learn to forgive, we are on our way to handling conflict in a mature manner.

HANDLING DIFFICULT SITUATIONS

In all our dealings with people, we are going to encounter difficult situations. Although you have 20 women who love attending, the one who didn't get her child into child care is the one who can throw you off balance. Being prepared is the best way to handle those difficult situations.

1. Be a good listener. Ask questions to find out what the real problem is. Often the problem stems from something at home or a difficult issue she is facing.
2. Give information that may help her understand the situation.
3. Help to resolve the situation if possible.
4. If it seems appropriate, offer to pray with her.

As representatives of our group, we must interact with women in a way that tells them they are important. Our communication must never be affected by our moods; rather, it must be based on the fruit of the Spirit: love, joy, peace, patience, kindness, gentleness, faithfulness, goodness, and self-control.

FROM MY ♥ TO YOURS

When a community of believers (and even unbelievers!) operates according to godly standards, a new depth of relationship takes place. An honest, safe environment is created and may be experienced for the first time in an individual's life. Regardless of how you have handled conflict in the past, handle it according to God's Word from here on out. These instructions are not only for relationships between moms but also between husband and wife and parent and child. There is no better way than God's way. I remember the first time I followed Matthew 18. I was so scared I was shaking. Now, many years later, I don't particularly enjoy the process, but I've learned to trust it, knowing that God's way is always the right way.

Chapter 18

Take Off Your Mask

When introducing ourselves at marriage conferences, my husband, Mark, and I often introduce ourselves as being married 19 years, 9 of them happily. As much as we wish that wasn't true, it is. However, by being honest right up front, we establish not only our credibility but also our ability to understand the intricacies of building a marriage. Simply put, we speak from experience.

Is it hard to be open about our "stuff"? Sure it is. But we need to realize that as humans we all experience similar struggles, emotions, and frustrations. It may be packaged a bit differently for each person, but the feelings, the hurts, and the freedom experienced when healing is found is essentially the same.

HONESTY BREEDS HONESTY

Mom2Mom was four years old. Still meeting in a home, we were bulging at the seams of the large living room where we met every week. I continued to serve as the facilitator for the group, leading discussions about the books we were reading together. Other leaders oversaw an occasional craft, the weekly refreshments, and our child-care program at a church just down the road.

This week's lesson was on marriage, and as discussion leader I was struggling. You see, Mark and I were at a difficult point in our marriage. We were seeing a counselor every week and truly at rock bottom in our relationship. The problem was that we looked good on the outside. Mark was a children's pastor in our large church. I was very visible leading the moms ministry and serving on the church's worship team. We painted a pretty good picture on the outside, but we were dying on the inside.

As I prayed about the upcoming discussion on marriage, I felt God prompting me to share honestly. "I can't," I responded to him in prayer. "If I do, it will affect our credibility as leaders. Not only that," I continued, "but it might jeopardize Mark's job." I finished my argument with, "I really don't want to air our dirty laundry with everyone else anyway."

By the time Wednesday arrived, I knew what I needed to do, and I was scared to death. God had won the argument (as he always does!), and I needed to be obedient. As we launched into the discussion of our assigned chapter that morning, I mustered up the courage to be honest. Raw emotion spilled into tears as I revealed the true condition of our marriage and that we were seeking professional help.

What happened next utterly surprised me. I saw tears in the eyes of many of the women in front of me. Some were tears of compassion, hurting because I hurt. Others were tears of empathy from women living with similar pain and frustrations in their marriages.

Over the next week the phone calls and letters I received from the moms in the group astounded me. Our marriage was not the only marriage in trouble. My honesty was breeding honesty in others as well.

HONESTY BUILDS TRUST

While my reservations about being honest were based on many fears, the truth not only took our group to a new level of relationship, but it also increased my integrity as a leader. No longer was I perceived to be the "perfect" wife and mom whom women could easily put on a pedestal; I was a fallible leader who wrestled with the same things as everyone else. I became trustworthy in their eyes; the honesty helped them be confident that I was the same person on the inside as I was on the outside.

HONESTY GIVES HOPE

Later, as I described some small victories we were experiencing in our marriage, the women in the group were encouraged. As I shared lessons that God was teaching me in this difficult season, the moms similarly were challenged. And as I gave testimony to the work God was doing in our relationship, those who were hurting experienced hope that their relationship could find healing also.

HONESTY HELPS HEAL

As long as we keep others in the dark about our sin, we will justify it, try to explain it away, blame it on someone else, and minimize it over and over in our minds. It is not until we are honest about our mistakes, calling them what they are—sins—that we truly will want to make a change. That's when we turn on the light, open up, and begin to experience freedom from the deception of the enemy.

RISKS AND WARNINGS

MISUSED INFORMATION. I have been "unmasked" for 14 years. I'm openly honest about where God is "growing me" and about what struggles I am facing. In those 14 years, I have never had negative feedback as a result of being transparent. However, there is always the risk that someone will take the information and misuse it in a judgmental or gossipy way. I believe it is a risk worth taking. I also believe that when a person does handle the information inappropriately, God gives us guidelines for handling that conflict.

Several years ago, a pastor and his wife were the subject of some very ugly rumors within the Christian community. They found out where the rumors had begun, and they decided to visit the influential person, set the record straight, and ask him to cease the gossip. They did not approach this person in anger, but with respect. The man was so caught off guard by their polite visit that he admitted his wrongdoing and apologized for believing things he had heard and using his influence to support the gossip.

FAMILY SENSITIVITIES. Another risk of being transparent is that of betraying your husband or children. You and I have the responsibilities of confidentiality not only as a leader but as a family member. We have to protect our family relationships and must not share something publicly about a member of the family unless we have his or her permission. We have to limit our transparency to what God is showing us personally.

When I was honest about my difficult marriage that first time in my moms group, I said I knew God was going to teach me a lot through the experience. Mark and I were struggling for a lot of reasons: criticism, anger, lack of conflict resolution skills, pornography, and more. However, at that time, I spoke only about what I was learning: that my criticism and judgment were damaging our relationship, that I needed to listen more than speak, and that I needed to learn more about God's plan for the physical relationship in marriage. I did not have the right or permission to "uncover" my husband in any way by disclosing his problems.

Now Mark and I speak frequently about our marriage. We teach marriage seminars and have told our story not only at a podium but even in a national magazine. We both are completely comfortable talking about our marriage openly, and we have given each other permission to share not only what we are learning but also what the other person is learning if we feel prompted to do so.

The same applies to our children. Our oldest daughter was 14 when we were asked to tell our marriage story in a feature article for *Today's Christian Woman* magazine. Part of our story concerns the baggage Mark and I both brought into our relationship not only from the homes in which we grew up but also as a result of the choices we had made—to be sexually active—in dating relationships before marriage.

Because we sensed that many couples were facing the same struggles, we wanted to address this in the article. We wanted to give hope and help by talking about the real issues of marriage. But to do that, we felt we needed to be honest with our children. Two of our children were too young to understand, but our 14-year-old daughter and 12-year-old son needed to know the truth if their mom and dad were going to talk openly about this subject.

Mark and I sat down with Anne and Evan to discuss the subject one evening. We had long before decided that if our kids asked us about our pasts, we would be honest, but if they never asked, we would not offer sensitive information. After sharing the truth as well as our opportunity to encourage other couples, Anne and Evan were quiet. Evan said that he thought it was okay and then asked if he could return to playing Nintendo. Anne, on the other hand, began to cry. We had disappointed her. She wasn't rattled about this opportunity to share; it was that this new information suddenly knocked us off the pedestal she had placed us on. She thought we were perfect (remember—she was just entering the teen years!), but, alas, we weren't. It took her several days to sort through her emotions, but eventually she brought the subject up and affirmed the opportunity to encourage so many readers. She realized the value of having an accurate picture of the incredible change God had made in our lives. Knowing we had made poor decisions in our early years, she sensed that her life was a direct result of God's grace.

DISCRETION. My kids have a saying they use now and then: "TMI"—Too Much Information; in other words, more than they want to know! When talking about our pasts with our children and with others, we want to give enough information to be honest but not so much that they can paint pictures in their minds. Certainly there are details that don't need to be enumerated. Use discretion; don't give too much information when it really isn't necessary. Maintain a balance when operating with honesty and openness.

Taking off your mask involves risks, but the rewards outweigh those risks. As my mother used to say: Honesty is the best policy.

FROM MY ♥ TO YOURS

It takes courage to be honest, but don't let the enemy make you believe that if you admit your mistakes and struggles you'll be respected less as a leader. Some sin issues require a sabbatical from ministry. At other times we need to let go of responsibilities to take time to heal from hurts and poor choices. In most circumstances, however, a leader who is honest and vulnerable is also a leader of integrity who is highly respected by those she leads.

Chapter 19

Lean into God

Several years ago, the Hearts at Home leadership team studied the book of Nehemiah. If you have never read the book of Nehemiah (found in the Old Testament), you might consider doing so. What encouragement we found there, as moms, wives, leaders, and children of God. Let's look at 12 transferable leadership principles culled from Nehemiah, who leaned into God as he led the people to rebuild the walls around Jerusalem. Some of these principles we have addressed in earlier chapters; others provide new perspectives. This material may be used in your personal study; it is also a wonderful way to keep God's Word foundational for your leadership team. Should you use part 3 of this book as a year's leadership curriculum for your team, you can also use these 12 principles from Nehemiah as another year's worth of leadership lessons.

START WITH GOD

When I started Mom2Mom, I felt strongly about my role as a mother and wanted to do it well. When God gave me the vision for a national Hearts at Home conference, the passion for my vision to encourage mothers grew even stronger. However, the task was so large that if I didn't partner with God, I was sure to fail.

In Nehemiah 1 we see Nehemiah greatly burdened by the fact that the walls of Jerusalem are broken down, making the city vulnerable to its enemies. He mourns and fasts and prays before God. In fact, most of chapter 1 is Nehemiah's prayer. In his prayer, we find three very important principles:

1. He recognizes God for who he is.
2. He confesses his own sin.
3. He is specific in asking God to help him.

This prayer was important because it included God in Nehemiah's plans, prepared Nehemiah's heart, and gave God room to work. As moms group leaders, we need to do the same.

TRUST GOD'S SELECTION

A simple verse at the end of Nehemiah 1 is very powerful, especially for moms. After Nehemiah pours out his heart to God, he says, "I was cupbearer to the king." Nehemiah did great things for God, but he was a nobody. He wasn't of noble descent; he didn't have a big, important, highly visible job. He was a simple man whose job was to give the king something to drink.

How many times do we say, "Oh, I could never do that!" when God asks us to do something? Maybe we back away from something God is calling us to do because we don't feel we have the experience or training. Nehemiah wasn't a wall builder, a construction worker, or even an experienced leader. When God calls us to do something, he provides all the training we need if we'll let him. God doesn't call the equipped; he equips the called.

PRACTICE PRAYING

Nehemiah wanted to go to Jerusalem to help rebuild the wall, but it required that he take a sabbatical from his job as cupbearer. To secure the leave, he needed to approach the king and ask for the time off. He not only asks for the time off, but also asks for the king's help in providing letters of recommendation to other leaders he would need to approach. Here is what is most striking about his request: "The king said to me, 'What is it you want?' Then I prayed to the God of heaven, and I answered the king . . ." (Neh. 2:4–5). These words hold a lesson for all of us. Nehemiah didn't speak without praying first. There will be many times when we as leaders need to make requests, give responses, and make decisions. We'll be tempted to do these things in our own strength, but God wants us to trust him for direction. If we stay in conversation with God all the time, we'll learn to lean into him more and more as we lead.

SHARE VISION

When God gives us a vision, he not only wants us to talk it over and over with him, he also wants us to share it with others. In Nehemiah 2:17, Nehemiah addresses the people by saying, "You see the trouble we are in: Jerusalem lies in ruins, and its gates have been burned with fire. Come, let us rebuild the wall of Jerusalem, and we will no longer be in disgrace." Nehemiah describes the problem and then casts the vision to solve it. This is the first step in inviting others to join you. Not only do we need to cast vision for the entire group, but every leader on your leadership team needs to understand the importance of casting vision for their area. The hospitality coordinator needs to cast vision in asking others to join her in welcoming the moms each week. The child-care coordinator casts vision for the importance of a quality children's program. When God plants an idea in your mind to accomplish something for him, share it with others and allow the Holy Spirit to work on them. You are inviting others to experience God in a faith journey.

TELL THE GOD STORIES

Nehemiah 2:18 says, "I also told them about the gracious hand of my God upon me and what the king had said to me." Up to this point, God had moved in some pretty incredible ways. Not only had the king given Nehemiah a leave of absence and the letters of recommendation as requested, but he also had provided army officers and a cavalry. God gave Nehemiah an armed escort to accompany him on the journey to Jerusalem! And Nehemiah testified of God's faithfulness to the people.

In verse 20 Nehemiah says, "The God of heaven will give us success." This is Nehemiah's way of saying, "This is God's gig!" That's what God wants us to do too. He wants us to remember that ministry is his work. Our job is to tell others of all he is doing. He wants us to tell of his mighty works. He wants us to talk about his faithfulness. When we have a front row seat at watching God work, let's make sure we tell others of his wonderful acts. You might even consider keeping a "God Story" journal for your group.

DELEGATE AND SHARE OWNERSHIP

Nehemiah 3:28 says, "Above the Horse Gate, the priests made repairs, each in front of his own house." In fact, throughout most of chapter 3 we read about different groups of people that accomplished different parts of the project. Nehemiah didn't want this to be his project alone. In having everyone work in front of his own home, ownership was established. This helped the people to be excited about their part in making the vision a reality.

Many leaders make the mistake of doing too much themselves. We have to learn to delegate, giving responsibility and ownership to others. If we don't, we rob them of the opportunity to experience God at work in their lives, and we are more likely to experience burnout.

RESIST DISCOURAGEMENT

Even in the midst of such an incredible project, Nehemiah ran into his share of naysayers. In Nehemiah 4 we read that Nehemiah and the Jews who were rebuilding the wall were taunted and ridiculed. Ministry is like that sometimes. When we step out in faith, some people will try to tell us the job is impossible. Anytime you are doing God's work, Satan will tell you that you can't do it.

The lesson we can learn here is based on how Nehemiah handled the discouragement. Again he prays to God, expressing his anger in prayer rather than by arguing back and taking matters into his own hands. God wants us to give everything to him, the good and the bad.

BLEND FAITH AND ACTION

Nehemiah learned of a plot against him, and he "prayed to . . . God and posted a guard day and night to meet this threat" (Neh. 4:9). Trusting God doesn't mean that we aren't responsible to do anything. It means we will trust him to direct us about what to do. Nehemiah blended faith with action, doing everything humanly possible and letting God take care of the rest.

When we work on a God-sized task, we need to work as if everything depends on us and pray as if everything depends on God.

RECAST VISION

After a season of hard work, the people of Judah came to Nehemiah and said, "The strength of the laborers is giving out, and there is so much rubble that we cannot rebuild the wall" (Neh. 4:10).

In a moms group, there will be times when a child-care leader is at the end of her rope, or when a care circle coordinator can't find enough leaders. This kind of discouragement is what we referred to earlier as mission drift (see p. 105). When this happens we need to recast the vision and build our leaders back up. We have to remind them of the importance of the job they are doing and share the God stories with them. Nehemiah did this by responding, "Remember the Lord, who is great and awesome, and fight for your brothers, your sons and your daughters, your wives and your homes" (4:14).

RESTRUCTURE WHEN NECESSARY

When Nehemiah heard that their enemies were plotting against them again, he restructured his plan. "From that day on, half of my men did the work, while the other half were equipped with spears, shields, bows and armor" (Neh. 4:16).

As a ministry grows and develops, some responsibilities will become too large for one person to carry. At this point it is necessary to rethink and restructure in order to spread the burden of responsibility. As my friend Karen says, "We need to slice, dice, and repackage this job!" This is especially important when working with volunteers, because we need to honor their time and family responsibilities. In other situations, we may need to rethink how we are doing something and try a new strategy that might work better. As leaders we can't be afraid of change. We need to prepare our people for it and help them navigate through it.

RESPOND RATHER THAN REACT

Sometimes people make poor choices and their actions affect others. This happened to Nehemiah when some of the Jews took advantage of their own people. When those who had been wronged came to Nehemiah with their complaint, he "pondered [it] in [his] mind" (Neh. 5:7) before he responded to the complaints by holding his leaders accountable. The leaders in turn agreed to give everything back.

If Nehemiah had reacted out of anger, the results would have been quite different. Nehemiah responded rather than reacted, and that is an important lesson for us to learn.

CELEBRATE AND APPRECIATE

The wall was completed in an amazing 52 days (Neh. 6:15). God did the impossible, and their skeptics were proven wrong. But Nehemiah didn't stop there. Eventually the people dedicated the wall and celebrated the accomplishment with a huge ceremony and party

(12:27–43). This affirmed the hard work and expressed appreciation for the sacrifices that had been made in the process. "The sound of rejoicing . . . could be heard far away" (12:43).

As leaders, we need to celebrate what God has done in us and through us. We need to thank those who have given over and above what was expected. Take your leaders to lunch or have a party at the end of the year. This speaks appreciation to the leaders and keeps them on board for many years to come.

FROM MY ❤ TO YOURS

The Bible is full of wisdom for leaders. This peek into the life of Nehemiah is just a small portion of what God wants to teach us through his Word. If you are not accustomed to reading the Bible, I ask you to consider making it a regular part of your day. As busy moms, we need to be grounded in God's truth and apply it to our lives and in our leadership roles. This is what will truly allow us to "lean into God." If you don't have a study Bible with commentaries to help you understand the context, consider investing in one or asking for one as a gift. When the Bible comes alive for you, you will want to share what you are learning with others. That is what moves a leader from good to great.

Chapter 20

Keep the Balance

One of the hardest things for a leader to do is to keep balance. Most leaders are task-oriented, driven-to-succeed, hard workers. They usually don't do something halfway; it's all the way or nothing. Many leaders are perfectionists, wanting to make sure that everything is done just right. And many of us are lone rangers, doing entirely too much on our own.

It won't do you one bit of good to encourage other families if your family is being neglected because you are spending too much time on your leadership responsibilities. You'll lose integrity as a leader, not to mention damage your marriage and family relationships.

From the voice of experience (my own), here are some strategies that will help you find and keep the balance.

A MAJOR AND A MINOR

Several years ago a dear friend explained to me the leadership strategy of having one major and one minor volunteer responsibility. This is a manageable mix that allows you to keep your primary focus on your home and family.

A major activity might be serving as a moms group leader or teaching Sunday school weekly. It's any activity that takes regular preparation time—several hours per week.

A minor activity is one for which you just need to show up, for example, helping in the school library one hour each week. It could also be something like playing the piano for church one Sunday a month.

Before jumping into another major or minor activity, consider resigning from the previous activity. If you don't set these boundaries, you will find yourself with too much on your plate, and you won't be doing anything well.

LEARN HOW TO SAY NO

It is imperative that you learn to say no to activities that will compromise your family. In my book *Professionalizing Motherhood*,[16] I share the following strategies for saying no.

1. REMEMBER THAT YOU, AS A STAY-AT-HOME MOM, ARE GOING TO BE ASKED TO VOLUNTEER MORE OFTEN, SIMPLY BECAUSE YOU ARE MORE AVAILABLE THAN OTHER WOMEN WITH LESS FLEXIBLE CALENDARS. With many mothers working outside the home, there are fewer school, church, and community volunteers available during the day. Keep this in mind and remember that you alone know what is best for your family.

2.   *NEVER SAY YES ON THE SPOT.* When your help is requested, always say you will call the person back after you have had time to pray and think about it. This keeps you from regretting a hasty decision. You may say no on the spot if you know immediately that the commitment is not right for you.

3.   *WHEN CONSIDERING A COMMITMENT, MAKE SURE YOU FACTOR IN PREPA-RATION TIME.* Most of us underestimate how long it takes to complete a job. If someone asks you to bake five dozen cookies, look at the calendar and determine whether you truly have that much free time available before the cookies need to be delivered. If your calendar looks too busy, say no.

4.   *WHEN CONSIDERING LONG-TERM COMMITMENTS, BE SURE TO FACTOR INTO YOUR SCHEDULE THE TIME REQUIRED TO FULFILL ALL YOUR HOUSEHOLD RESPONSIBILITIES.* You may think that becoming the president of an organization you strongly believe in will not take all that much time, but months down the road, will phone calls, meetings, and errands cut into the time you previously used for laundry, house-cleaning, or paying the bills? These are big household jobs that need to be considered in your weekly and daily calendar. Don't allow your family responsibilities to be sacrificed for your volunteer responsibilities.

5.   *REMEMBER TO CONSIDER THE "BRAIN SPACE" A NEW RESPONSIBILITY WILL TAKE.* Have you ever been listening to your children but really thinking about a new project or the hundreds of things you need to do? When your mind is cluttered, you are not mentally available to your family.

6.   *REMEMBER THAT EVERY MINUTE OF YOUR DAY DOES NOT HAVE TO BE SCHEDULED.* If you have a "doer" mentality, you will think of a spare hour or two as a way to fit in one more yes. In reality we need time to do nothing. If this is hard for you, consider scheduling in "downtime" each day. Write it on your calendar and say no to anything that would jeopardize that time.

7.   *SET A LIMIT TO THE NUMBER OF LONG-TERM COMMITMENTS YOU WILL CARRY.* As I noted above, I have (and recommend) one large and one small long-term volunteer commitment. By limiting your long-term commitments, you have more time to help out in short-term service projects—baking brownies for your child's classroom or being a teacher's assistant during vacation Bible school.

8.   *ASK FOR ACCOUNTABILITY.* Ask your husband, a close friend, or your Bible study group to hold you accountable for the number of commitments you will carry. Be open to that person's insight. If you have trouble saying no, ask this person to help you while you

get things back in balance. When someone asks for a commitment and you say you will call her back, check with your accountability partner before making that call. Sort through your schedule with her. Eventually you won't need her help, but it can help you get on your feet as you learn to say no.

9. *DON'T FEEL THAT YOU NEED TO GIVE A LONG LIST OF EXCUSES.* You know what is best for your family and for yourself. If you feel you need to give an excuse, simply say that it would not fit into your schedule at this time.

10. *KEEP IN MIND THAT YOU DO NOT HAVE TO SAY YES SIMPLY BECAUSE YOU ARE CAPABLE.* You may have strong leadership skills and most likely will be asked to lead most anything you are involved in. That doesn't mean you have to say yes to those responsibilities. You say yes only after considering your family commitments, your passion for the organization, your time availability, other volunteer responsibilities, and what you may need to give up to properly do the job.

11. *IF YOU HAVE TOO MUCH ON YOUR PLATE NOW, EVALUATE YOUR PRIORITIES.* Determine what responsibilities you need to let go. Give one month's notice to organizations for which you will no longer be able to serve. Although it may be difficult to give up a responsibility, you are not doing the organization or your family any good when you cannot fully commit to the job. As soon as you let go of the responsibilities you were carrying, instill new boundaries into your thoughts. Don't let yourself become overcommitted again. Saying no allows others the opportunity to say yes.

12. *REMEMBER THAT SAYING YES TO SOME ACTIVITIES OUTSIDE THE HOME WILL BE IMPORTANT TO YOUR SANITY.* Moms of young children especially need to get out of the house to socialize and think about something other than diapers, bottles, and coupons. But we need to choose carefully what to be involved in so as to use our time wisely. You will be amazed at the patience you will have with your family when you find balance in your activity schedule.

DOING AND BEING

God is far more concerned about the condition of our hearts than what we are doing for him. He wants us to spend time with him, keeping a margin in our lives so that we have space for whatever he may ask us to do in a day. Don't be a "human doing." You are a "human being."

As leaders, we easily become so task oriented that we miss out on the relational opportunities around us. Don't forget to figure in time this week to have a friend over, take your kids to the park, write a letter, or go on a date with your husband. We don't usually schedule these activities, but they are the first to go when we are overcommitted.

ORGANIZATIONAL TIPS

USE TECHNOLOGY. If you have voice mail or an answering machine, use it! Use it when you are home to give your family uninterrupted time. Don't answer calls during meals or while reading your child a book. Let the machine kick in when you are having a good conversation with your husband. The phone does not have to control your life. Determine when it is the best time to talk, and return calls accordingly.

Use email whenever possible. The best thing about email communication is that it is done on your own time. Composing, sending, reading, and answering messages can be done when *you* have the time to do it. Don't be obsessed with email; check it once or twice a day and enjoy the freedom of this flexible form of communication.

GET CREATIVE. Organize your volunteer activities with notebooks, folders, files, or whatever will help you to keep information together. When you are ready to work on a project, it will be easy to find. Depending on the size of your responsibilities, you may want to use a desk-top file organizer or a file cabinet drawer.

Don't depend completely on your computer hard drive. Make sure you back up important documents to save you time, energy, and grief should your computer crash.

Keep copies of your moms group phone list or directory next to every phone in your home. This will help when you need to make a phone call while folding the laundry or doing some other chore. Multitask when possible.

DELEGATE OFTEN. If you have 20 phone calls to make, ask someone to take half of the list. If you need to stuff envelopes, ask two friends over to help you. If someone else can do the job, let her! If the job can be shared, set up a time to work together. This principle is not only efficient, but it also encourages relationship building.

FAMILY PRIORITIES

When you are working as a volunteer, it is especially important that your family feels that they are a higher priority than the task on which you are working. One way to show your priority is by practicing face-to-face communication—making eye contact. If you are sitting at your computer, working on a document for your moms group, and your son comes in to ask you a question, stop what you are doing, turn your body toward him, and respond with full eye contact. This says, "I value you. You are more important than what I'm working on."

PRAY

Commit your day to the Lord, and he will help you accomplish what needs to be accomplished for the day.

FROM MY ♥ TO YOURS

I have had seasons of ministry when my life was very balanced. In these seasons the laundry got done, evening meals were on the table most nights, and there was a sense of calm in our home. There have been other seasons when I have felt that my children and husband were interruptions to what I was doing. That was a big clue that my life was out of balance.

Keep your priorities in order. The ministry you do in your home is far more important than any ministry you will ever do outside the home.

Part 4

The Church Connection

Chapter 21

Moms Ministry:
An Effective Church Outreach

Dear Hearts at Home,

I am a stay-at-home, homeschooling mom who is very overwhelmed with the responsibilities of "doing it all." I have no mom, no siblings, and no support. I am always meeting everyone's needs and now find myself feeling exhausted and frustrated because none of my needs are ever met. My in-laws are nonsupportive, so I feel all alone, with the whole world on my shoulders.

I really need some support. Can you help me?

Signed,
A Mom with a Heavy Heart

We received this email while I was writing the manuscript for this book. The desperation this mother feels is not uncommon. She feels as if she is drowning; she hopes that someone will throw her a life vest. She mentions nothing of faith, leaving us to assume it may not be a priority for her. She is the average mom who is looking for help in her job as a wife and mother. Will it be your church that reaches out to her?

AN EFFECTIVE OUTREACH TOOL

As a member of the worship team standing in the front of our church one Sunday, I became very aware of the faces in front of me. I scanned the room from left to right and counted more than two dozen families sitting in the service that had made this their church home after the mother had become involved in Mom2Mom. About half of those families were unchurched before they were introduced to faith through Mom2Mom.

A moms ministry is one of the strongest outreach programs a church can have. Most mothers of young children are searching for encouragement. They want answers to the difficulties of parenting and the challenges of marriage. They are motivated for self-improvement, looking to be better equipped as wives, mothers, and homemakers. What happens when an unchurched mom begins attending a church-sponsored moms group? A whole new world opens up to her!

COMFORT LEVEL INCREASES

Some moms will attend a moms group at a church when they wouldn't ever consider attending a Sunday service. This is because the group addresses their felt needs. They feel understood. Friendships replace loneliness. When Mom starts attending a moms group, she becomes comfortable in the church building. She begins to recognize some of the people who attend or work there. This makes the option of coming to Sunday morning church services far more appealing.

UNEXPECTED EVANGELISM OPPORTUNITIES

Sometimes churches are intentional about making their facilities available for community events. The premise is that these events give opportunity for the unchurched to visit the building; they may even be prompted to try a Sunday service. The same principle applies to a moms group that meets in a church building.

When considering a moms ministry, we usually think about the impact this group will have on the mother who will attend as well as her family. However, there are others we have the opportunity to influence too.

Speakers or special guests who set up a display or come to talk about a community event may benefit from visiting the moms group. If your group sponsors special programs such as Home Improvement Day or Pamper Me Day, you have an opportunity to reach out to the demonstrators.

You will also have the opportunity to be the hands and feet of Jesus to child-care workers as you show interest in them, appreciate them, and reach out to them. If your child-care program hires college students, they may be searching for God's touch on their lives just like the mother who attends the program. When they are in the church building each week, they begin to feel comfortable and may even be intrigued by the church's resources or college ministry. If you hire from the community at large, the outreach opportunities will be similar as workers grow more knowledgeable of the church and its ministries.

LIFESTYLE EVANGELISM OPPORTUNITIES ABOUND

One Wednesday morning after our moms group finished up, Terry waited to talk to me. As I exited the building, she approached me and asked if I had a few moments to chat. Terry had been attending Mom2Mom for several months, and although she was consistent in her attendance, she was quiet most of the time.

We sat down on a park bench to talk while the kids played on the church playground. Terry began to unfold her story. She confessed that she was unhappy in her motherhood, in her marriage, and in her life in general. Finally, Terry said, "Bottom line, Jill: I want what you have. How can I get it?"

The laughter, the sense of camaraderie, the honesty and openness of our time on Wednesday mornings sometimes included allusions to faith, but more often it centered around motherhood issues. All the while Terry was watching, and she sensed something different. The seeds had been planted, and now was the time of harvest. I had the opportunity to share with Terry God's beautiful plan of salvation and his design for her to live in relationship with him. As we sat on that bench outside the church, Terry accepted Jesus Christ as her Savior.

TRUTH IS INTRODUCED

We live in a world that has no sense of right and wrong. Moral relativism abounds with its message that truth is based on how you feel about something. The world says that what is true for one person may not be true for another. God's plan, however, involves absolute truth, absolute right and wrong. Absolute truth is the black and white in our gray world.

When an unbelieving mom is saturated in the world's messages, her actions impact the entire family. However, when she is drawn to a moms group where many of her needs are met as a mother, she has the opportunity to hear about God's truth—maybe for the first time in her life. She also sees women who live with a filter of faith that intrigues her. She sees a peace in their lives and yearns for that in her life as well. Slowly truth begins to permeate and change her heart.

Tonya had been attending Mom2Mom for several years. She was a sweet woman with a sensitive heart, but she had never made a decision for God. One day Tonya asked me how to battle her low self-esteem because she was always dealing with negative thoughts about herself. It was as if there were tapes in her head playing all the time, telling her how stupid she was.

I suggested that she pick up Neil Anderson's book *Victory over the Darkness*[17] to see if it could help her understand the battle waging in her mind. Tonya later told me that she went right to the bookstore and bought the book. She headed to the gym to work out and set the book on the handlebars of a stationary bike and read as she pedaled. She read Anderson's explanation of God's plan of salvation, and she knew—right there in the gym—that this was where she needed to start. She accepted Christ sitting on that stationary bike, oblivious to those around her.

Tonya began a journey of healing that eventually made a powerful impact on her unbelieving husband. About a year later he also accepted the Lord. Now 10 years later they are in full-time ministry, planting a new church.

When moms are introduced to truth, their lives change. Truth is bound to make a difference in their families. A church with a ministry to moms will see membership growth as these women who influence their families take God's truth home. Dr. Brenda Hunter puts it well in her book *What Every Mother Needs to Know:* "If you help a mother love her life, you will help a family. And as families go, so goes society."[18] That is the power of evangelism through a moms ministry.

FROM MY ♥ TO YOURS

Many church leaders do not value women's ministries as an evangelism tool. Quite honestly, it is because most church leaders are not women and don't understand firsthand the dynamics of women's relationships. A moms ministry is an incredibly valuable outreach opportunity. It's a very wide back door to the church. If you don't know where to find money to support a moms ministry in your church, check out the missions/evangelism budget. You just may find that a moms ministry will give an incredible return on the investment. Because when you invest in a mother, you influence a family. When you influence a family, you improve a community. And when you improve a community, you impact the world!

Chapter 22

What Does This Group Need from Our Church?

In 14 years of leading a moms ministry and serving as a consultant to new and existing groups, I have learned that the most difficult part of leading a moms group isn't finding volunteers. It isn't finding qualified child-care workers. It's not even organizing 15 to 20 speakers each year. The biggest challenge most moms group leaders face is securing the encouragement and support of church leadership for this incredibly valuable outreach ministry.

What does a moms group need from a church? The list is short, but it is central to the success of the group.

MORAL SUPPORT

No amount of budget monies speaks encouragement like good old-fashioned moral support. Knowing that the church leaders believe in the ministry, value its mission, and pray for it on a regular basis will fuel the passion of a moms group leader more than anything else.

As a church, your interest and promotion will give confirmation and credibility to the ministry. As a church leader, your personal investment—helping to set up tables and chairs or copying handouts on occasion—will affirm and empower the leadership team of the moms group.

An occasional handwritten note from the pastor or chairman of the elders to the moms group director will help her feel appreciated and valued. A visit once or twice a year to the group, to welcome them to the church, will validate the ministry and its connection to the larger church family. This first line of support doesn't cost anything other than time and energy.

The pastors of one church I know stand at the door and in the parking lot to help moms as they arrive. If it's raining, they rush out to the car with an umbrella. If it's snowing, they have the moms pull up to the door, help the moms unload babies and toddlers, and then offer to park their cars. Sometimes a mom has to carry an infant seat and a diaper bag while navigating a busy parking lot with two preschoolers. What an opportunity for the church staff to be the hands and feet of Jesus when a mom needs them most!

FACILITY USE

Regardless of size, most moms groups need a facility in which to meet. A small group may need the use of one classroom each week. A larger ministry may need every square foot of available classroom and nursery space one morning a week. A willingness to open the church facility to a program that will bring women from the community into your building is essential.

Clearly defined guidelines for the facility usage will circumvent problems later on. Items to consider are:

- When can setup take place? The night before? The morning of?
- Who will set up the tables and chairs? Whose job is it to tear them down?
- Will janitorial staff clean the rooms after they are used, or will the moms group be responsible for taking out trash, vacuuming, wiping off tables, etc.?
- Can the kitchen be used? Coffeemakers? Serving dishes?
- Will rooms be unlocked, or does someone need to be given a key?
- If setup takes place the night before, will the building be unlocked for the setup crew, or does someone need to have a master key?
- What about A/V equipment? Are there any TV/VCR/DVDs available? Where can they be found? What about sound equipment, if needed?
- Will the children's programming have access to children's craft supplies like scissors, glue, paper, etc.?
- Is there a place where the moms group can store supplies, such as cups, plates, napkins, tablecloths, lending library, etc.?

ADMINISTRATIVE ASSISTANCE

Most effective moms groups will produce a variety of communication documents. Brochures, letters, speaker handouts, newsletters, announcement sheets, phone directories—these are some of the items a moms group may need to create and duplicate. Most groups have the ability to create the documents but will need to have access to a copy machine. If your church's machine requires a user's code, consider giving the moms group a code. Empower the group to minister effectively. If you only allow the church secretary to use the copy machine, prepare her for the extra workload. In this scenario, it may also be necessary to clarify the need for communication about upcoming projects. A work order sheet may be submitted to request administrative help.

A group that is just starting may require limited administrative assistance. If the group grows, the church should adjust its services as needed.

FINANCIAL SUPPORT

Smaller moms ministries will require little financial support from a church budget. Larger, more organized ministries may necessitate some financial investment. For instance, if a church decides to sponsor a MOPS group, the church serves as the chartered organization and agrees to oversee the financial liability of the ministry. Ideally, a church will support a moms ministry through its budget, in a missions, Christian education, or women's ministry category.

Some churches have extended financial support by providing tangible items, such as cups, plates, napkins, coffee, or children's curriculum. Administrative supplies such as paper, name tags, and postage may also be provided by the church. Some churches also budget monies to help subsidize child-care expenses in order to keep fees affordable for one-income moms.

A LOVING ATTITTUDE

As the moms group uses the facility, invariably mistakes will be made along the way. An attitude of grace, patience, love, and forgiveness will keep relationships intact and preserve the dignity of those serving. To a volunteer, there's nothing worse than getting in trouble for doing something you didn't even know was wrong. (That's the voice of experience speaking!) As a church, you can support a volunteer-run ministry by making sure expectations are stated up front and mistakes are corrected with love and grace. When approaching a volunteer about a problem, give the benefit of the doubt—that she didn't know what she did wasn't the right way to do it. Rather than criticizing, be sensitive and kind when clarifying the issue. Then work to bring resolution to the problem while affirming her hard work for the kingdom.

FROM MY ♥ TO YOURS

I love to watch God expand a vision and grow a ministry. He takes our limited abilities and expands them beyond our imaginations. When we step out in faith, we truly have a front seat to watch God work.

My prayer is that you, as a church family, will do everything possible to fully support the vision and excitement of the moms in your church who want to educate, encourage, and equip women in the profession of motherhood.

Appendix A

Professional Resources for Mothers at Home

HEARTS AT HOME

Hearts at Home Conferences and Resources

Hearts at Home Magazine

Hearts at Home Devotional

Hearts at Home
900 W. College Ave.
Normal, IL 61761
309-888-MOMS
www.hearts-at-home.org

OTHER ORGANIZATIONS FOR MOTHERS

MOPS International (Mothers of Preschoolers)
2370 S. Trenton Way
Denver, CO 80231-3822
888-910-MOPS
www.mops.org

National Association of At-Home Mothers
405 E. Buchanan Ave.
Fairfield, IA 52556
www.athomemothers.com

MOCAH (Mothers of Color at Home)
P.O. Box 188
Union City, GA 30291

Home and Family Network
9493–C Silver King Court
Fairfax, VA 22031
703-352-1072
www.familyandhome.org

Moms In Touch
P.O. Box 1120
Poway, CA 92074
501-223-8663
www.momsintouch.org

Proverbs 31 Ministry
616–G Matthews–Mint Hill Road
Matthews, NC 28105
877-P31-HOME
www.gospelcom.net/p31

Sweet Monday
10001 Patterson Ave. Suite 204
Richmond, VA 23233
804-754-4333
www.sweetmonday.com

Sample Job Descriptions and Responsibilities

LEADERSHIP

DIRECTOR

I. Visionary
   A. Present new or improved ideas.
   B. Set direction for the ministry team.
   C. Set spiritual direction.
II. Administrator
   A. Lead all leadership team meetings.
      1. Prepare agenda ahead of time.
      2. Ensure that a quality amount of time is spent in prayer.
      3. Guide evaluation.
      4. Guide planning.
   B. Lead all moms group meetings.
      1. Schedule activities of the day.
      2. Make announcements.
      3. Lead prayer.
   C. Staff all leadership positions.
   D. Place book orders with local bookstore if needed.
   E. Communicate with assistant director to evaluate and plan.
   F. Communicate with church leadership.
      1. Reserve rooms through the administrative assistant.
      2. Communicate with women's ministry director.
   G. Arrange advertising.
      1. Church newsletter.
      2. Church bulletin.
      3. Newspaper.

ASSISTANT DIRECTOR

I.   Assist director on meeting days.
    A. Arrive half hour early for meetings.
    B. Check with director to see what needs to be done.
II.   Communicate to the director if supplies are needed.
III. In absence of the leader, lead meetings.
IV. Attend all leadership meetings.
V.   Help with anything needed throughout week.
VI. Coordinate and oversee summer mailing for preregistration.

CARE CIRCLE COORDINATOR

I.   Recruit and train care circle leaders.
II.   Coordinate all women into a care circle according to the ages of their children (or neighborhood or ...).
III. Create folder for each circle leader and include an attendance sheet for each folder.
IV. Schedule care circles to provide moms' snack/facility setup/cleanup/child care, as appropriate. Include schedule(s) in handbook.
V.   Coordinate with hospitality coordinator to assign new moms to appropriate care circles.
VI. Keep in touch with care circle leaders to encourage them and identify any concerns or problems.
VII. Attend monthly leadership meetings.

DIRECTOR OF CHILD CARE

(See job description in children's program section, p. 160.)

CRAFT COORDINATOR

I.   Organize meetings with craft team. Brainstorm and plan crafts for designated craft days.
    A. Prepare sample crafts to show and display to whole group three weeks prior to craft day.
    B. Make any precraft preparations or delegate preparations to craft team (e.g., cut material ahead of time, paint or stain wood, etc.).
II.   Announce each craft and briefly explain how to make each craft three weeks before craft day.
    A. Prepare craft sign-up sheet with a list of all craft choices and cost.
    B. Collect money for crafts two weeks and one week prior to craft day.
    C. Purchase all materials needed for all crafts.

III. Help organize the setup of the meeting room for craft day.
   A. Organize craft team members to demonstrate/teach a craft on craft day.
   B. Send thank-you notes to anyone donating time, supplies, or skills to support craft days.
   C. Clean up all craft supplies.
IV. Keep inventory of craft supplies.
V. Before the semester begins, design and create a name-tag board and bulletin board.
VI. Create name tags for the group. These can be created before the first meeting or can be created by the moms at the first meeting.
VII. Attend monthly leadership meetings.

FACILITIES COORDINATOR

I. Before the semester begins, see that signs are made for each child-care room, directions to main meeting room, care circle numbers, and any other signs needed in the main meeting room.
II. Make sure there is a setup/cleanup list in each room and it is up-to-date.
III. Train child-care teachers and care circle leaders about setup and cleanup in their areas before the semester begins.
IV. Arrive a half hour early on the morning of the meeting to see that all the rooms are being (or have been) set up appropriately.
V. Check all rooms after the meeting is over to make sure they have been cleaned properly. All rooms must be returned to the same or better condition. All supplies must be returned to the proper storage areas.
VI. Attend all monthly leadership meetings.

FINANCIAL COORDINATOR

I. Get list of active moms from the hospitality or child registration coordinator.
   A. Record payment for child-care and activity fees.
   B. Organize extra help when collecting child-care fees. These helpers will be your team.
II. Buy any supplies that you may need (e.g., envelopes for paying workers).
III. Check with child-care team to get a list of workers and how much they are paid.
IV. Serve as the accountant/bookkeeper for the group.
V. Provide financial report at each leadership team meeting.
   A. Weekly responsibilities.
      1. Collect money at morning meetings (child care, craft, activity fee, etc.). The team leader should arrive by 8:15 A.M. Team members should arrive by 8:45 A.M.

2. Pay child-care workers for previous week worked.
3. Make sure all workers sign in.
V. Attend all monthly leadership meetings.
VI. Work closely with Fundraising Coordinator.

FUNDRAISING COORDINATOR

I. Coordinate fundraising events.
II. Call and schedule events.
III. Recruit volunteers to work events.
IV. Work closely with Financial Coordinator.
V. Attend all monthly leadership meetings.

HOSPITALITY COORDINATOR

I. Delegate team duties.
II. Oversee new member registration.
III. Work with care circle coordinator to assign walk-ins to a care circle.
IV. Keep supply box stocked at the registration desk.
V. Give moms' registration cards to care circle coordinator.
VI. Give children's registration cards to child registration coordinator.
VII. Organize schedule for greeters and takers.
VIII. Train greeters, takers, and occasionally entire membership about meeting new people.
IX. Attend all monthly leadership meetings.

LENDING LIBRARY COORDINATOR

I. Add books and tapes to library.
   A. Collect donated books and tapes.
   B. Periodically solicit publishers and authors for free resources.
   C. Add new materials to library.
      1. Create check-out cards.
      2. Attach category/author sticker to binding of book.
      3. Place in appropriate category in cabinet or on cart.
   D. Order supplies when needed (especially Hearts at Home tapes and videos).
   E. Reorder lost or damaged materials when needed.
   F. Inventory twice a year (Christmas and summer).
II. Oversee checkout during meeting.
   A. Be sure sheet of self-instructions are understandable and in a visible place.
   B. Check in returned materials.

C. Call people who have overdue materials.

D. If necessary, schedule workers to help on meeting days.

III. Attend monthly leadership meetings.

NEWSLETTER COORDINATOR

I. Coordinate collection, word processing, design, editing, and organization of newsletter.

II. Maintain due dates for collection of information and submission to church office for copying (or printing) to assure newsletter is distributed on time.

III. Follow up with committee leaders to include information about all upcoming events.

IV. Attend monthly leadership meetings.

PROGRAM COORDINATOR

I. Set up schedule of meetings—consider school holidays.

II. Select program topics.

III. Contact all speakers/leaders; greet and introduce them at the meeting.

IV. Reserve all audio or visual equipment needed for speakers.

V. Request check for speaker's fee or travel expenses from Financial Coordinator.

VI. Write a thank-you note to all speakers/leaders.

VII. Organize discussion group questions.

VIII. Plan and organize special events, such as an end-of-year banquet.

IX. Attend all monthly leadership meetings.

CARE CIRCLE LEADER

I. Make new members welcome.

A. Serve as a personal hostess for any new moms in your group. Introduce newcomers to the other members in your circle.

B. Contact each new circle member within two days of attending her first meeting.

1. Phone call.

2. Postcard.

II. Care for others in your group.

A. Explain the support system to your group. If they have a need they call you.

B. Take attendance and contact moms who are absent.

III. Facilitate discussions when needed (questions may be provided by speaker).

IV. Serve as point person when your care circle is in charge of snacks or setup/cleanup.

V.   Organize outings for your care circles occasionally (i.e., movie night, dinner at local restaurant, etc.).

CHILD-CARE PROGRAM — LEADERSHIP TEAM

DIRECTOR OF CHILD CARE

I.   Oversee and recruit the following leaders:
   A. Child registration coordinator
   B. Curriculum and snack coordinator
   C. Personnel coordinator
   D. Room mother coordinator
   E. Supply and toy coordinator
   F. Floor supervisor

II.   Hold monthly meetings with the above coordinators to evaluate child care.

III. Attend all leadership meetings to represent child care.

IV. Pray regularly for child care, teachers and assistants, volunteers, and coordinators.

V.   Send notes of encouragement to coordinators at least once a semester.

VI. Communicate with mothers regularly concerning child-care issues.

VII. Handle any questions, problems, or upset mothers if necessary.

VIII. Contact coordinators every other week to make sure things are running well.

IX. Help recruit for various teams and help coordinators to delegate appropriately.

CHILD-CARE COORDINATOR DEADLINE CALENDAR

May: Pray.

Fill all coordinator positions for the following year.

Schedule, send meeting reminders, and hold organizational meeting for coordinators.

June/July: Pray.

Attend any leadership meetings.

August: Pray.

Help with summer mailing, especially with child-care information being sent out.

Curriculum, child registration, and personnel coordinators all begin working.

Begin meeting monthly with child-care coordinators. (As the child-care coordinator, you will most likely have two meetings each month: one serving on the moms group leadership team and the other leading the child care.

Plan meeting schedule for entire year to give to team.

September: Pray.

Help organize child-care information from preregistration mailing.

Room mom coordinator, setup and cleanup coordinator, supply and toy coordinator, and floor supervisor kick into gear.

Stay in touch every other week with coordinators; help them when needed.

Communicate with mothers regularly concerning child-care issues.

October: Pray

Send notes of encouragement to coordinators; August and September are usually rough months.

Stay in touch every two weeks with coordinators; help them when needed.

Communicate with mothers regularly concerning child-care issues.

Help recruit for various teams, and help coordinators delegate appropriately.

Attend monthly child-care and leadership meetings.

November: Pray.

Stay in touch every two weeks with coordinators; help them when needed.

Communicate with mothers regularly concerning child care issues.

Help recruit for various teams, and help coordinators delegate appropriately.

Attend monthly child-care and leadership meetings.

December: Pray.

Again send notes of encouragement and thanks to team coordinators.

Remind them to send notes to those who serve on their teams.

Take a break—you deserve it!

January: Pray.

Registration and personnel coordinators begin working again.

Attend monthly child-care and leadership meetings.

February: Pray.

Stay in touch every two weeks with coordinators; help them when needed.

Communicate with mothers regularly concerning child-care issues.

Help recruit for various teams and help coordinators delegate appropriately.

Attend monthly child-care and leadership meetings.

March: Pray.

Stay in touch every two weeks with coordinators; help them when needed.

Communicate with mothers regularly concerning child-care issues.

Help recruit for various teams and help coordinators delegate appropriately.

Attend monthly child-care and leadership meetings.

April: Pray.

Stay in touch every two weeks with coordinators; help them when needed.

Communicate with mothers regularly concerning child-care issues.

Help recruit for various teams and help coordinators delegate appropriately.

Begin recruiting information for next year. Check with all coordinators to learn their plans for continuing in leadership.

Attend monthly child-care and leadership meetings.

Evaluate and make changes for next year.

May: Pray.

Send notes of thanks and encouragement to your coordinators.

Begin all over again! Congratulations on a great year!

CHILD REGISTRATION COORDINATOR

I.   Pray regularly for your job and your team.
II. Attend all child-care coordinator meetings.
III. Recruit a child registration team and delegate duties.
IV. Determine meeting needs for child registration team and schedule needed meetings.
V.   Possible delegation to team members:
     A. Room assignments and attendance.
     B. Name tags and ID numbers that match mother to child.
     C. Waiting list: bookkeeping and integration.

VI. Assign children to age-appropriate rooms, keeping track of worker-child ratios and promoting between semesters when needed.
VII. Communicate the number of children registered in various age groups to personnel coordinator and curriculum coordinator.
VIII. Make name tags for all children and place on boards or in boxes.
IX. Maintain waiting list through the year and determine when children can be added to classes.
X. Develop room attendance sheets. Keep track of attendance.
XI. Staff the registration table weekly to handle walk-ins or get new-child registration cards from hospitality team.

CURRICULUM AND SNACK COORDINATOR

I. Recruit a curriculum team if needed and delegate duties.
   A. Possible ways to delegate:
      1. Snack coordinator: snack shower, storage, distribution.
      2. Curriculum development.
      3. Curriculum distribution.
II. Work closely with registration coordinator to determine classroom numbers for crafts.
III. Interact with the teachers and workers.
IV. Review child-care classroom schedule each August and make any changes necessary for handbooks.
V. Plan curriculum topics for the year. Provide lesson plans at least one week in advance so teachers can prepare.
VI. Each week provide:
   A. Story or lesson
   B. Craft
   C. Video
   D. Snack
VII. Use the resource center appropriately.
VIII. Communicate snack shower needs and store snacks in closet.
IX. Distribute snacks and curriculum on the morning of each meeting a half hour before the meeting begins.
X. Plan and organize bathroom breaks.
XI. Send notes of encouragement to team members at least once a semester.
XII. Pray regularly for your job and your team.
XIII. Attend all child-care coordinator meetings.
XIV. Determine meeting needs for curriculum team and schedule needed meetings.

PERSONNEL COORDINATOR

I.   Pray regularly for your job and your team.

II.   Attend all child-care coordinator meetings.

III.   Recruit a personnel team or assistant and delegate duties.

IV.   Determine meeting needs for personnel team and schedule needed meetings.

V.   Work with registration coordinator to determine staff needs—teachers and assistants.

VI.   Hire child-care staff.

    A.   Run ads in newspapers and church bulletin.

    B.   Use recruitment video.

    C.   Send applications.

    D.   Interview (by phone or in person).

    E.   Check references and run background checks.

    F.   Assign to rooms and position.

VII.   Plan, communicate, and lead child-care training each semester (all other coordinators should also be involved in training).

VIII.   Hire 5 to 7 substitutes, if possible. Print a list of workers weekly for sign-in and sign-out—for financial team and for floor supervisor.

    A.   Sit at sign-in table to make sure all teachers and assistants show up.

    B.   Deal with no-shows strictly.

    C.   Handle any necessary dismissals with professionalism and in writing.

IX.   Provide financial team coordinator with addresses of all workers.

X.   Print list of workers wanting additional child-care work in monthly newsletter as soon as possible.

XI.   Secure substitutes as needed. If necessary, move workers around to maintain your established child-teacher ratios.

XII.   Send notes of encouragement and thanks to your team once a semester.

XIII.   Very important: Be in regular communication with your workers. Keep staff by taking care of them. Workers can be presented with a thank-you note and plate of cookies each December and given a thank-you gift each May.

ROOM MOTHER COORDINATOR

Purpose: It is helpful to have a mother on both sides of the door in each classroom when children are arriving and leaving. This allows the teachers and workers to work with the children as they arrive and leave. Room mothers are natural liaisons with teachers and can communicate needs or problems if necessary. Room mothers also take care of laundry if necessary.

I. Pray regularly for your job and your team of room mothers.
II. Attend all child-care coordinator meetings.
III. Determine meeting needs for room mothers' team and schedule orientation meeting and any other needed meetings.
IV. Recruit one or two room mothers per room and train appropriately.
V. Send notes of appreciation to room mothers once a semester.
VI. Handle room mother substitutions and recruitment throughout the semester.
VII. Follow up on room mothers who are not fulfilling their responsibilities.

SUPPLY AND TOY COORDINATOR

I. Pray regularly for your job.
II. Attend all child-care coordinator meetings.
III. Work with curriculum coordinator and determine supplies needed in the supply box of each room.
IV. Keep each room stocked with supply lists and pick up at checkout table each week.
V. Explain the supply lists to the teachers at orientation.
VI. Check boxes every other week to organize and restock.
VII. Keep regular stock of frequently used items (e.g., wipes, glue sticks, paper towels, Kleenex, etc.) in moms group storage area.
VIII. Keep blank Care Forms stocked in folders in each room.

CHILD-CARE PROGRAM—KEY WORKERS AND VOLUNTEERS

CHILD-CARE TEACHER

Time: 8:15–11:30 A.M., Wednesdays—September through May

I. Assess room conditions:
   A. Water
   B. Snack
   C. Curriculum
   D. Craft
II. Assist child-care workers in receiving children from room mothers.
III. Fill out attendance charts for children.
IV. Keep room on schedule.
V. Prepare activity for gym (if available).
VI. Lead craft time and story time.
VII. Direct cleanup:

A. Vacuum.
B. Wash tables and counters.
C. Put everything away (supplies and toys).
D. Take out trash.
E. Give used sheets, changing pads, etc. to room mother.
VIII. Return children to parent or guardian: Check all ID security numbers and remove name tags.

CHILD-CARE WORKERS

Time: 8:30–11:15 A.M., Wednesdays—September through May

I.   Receive children from room mothers.
   A.   Hang diaper bag with Care Form.
   B.   Check directions for care.
   C.   Interact with child.
II.   Take directions from teacher for day's activities.
III. Move TV/VCR and curriculum box to next room when finished (2-year-olds and up).
IV.   Change diapers and/or take children to restroom.
V.   Give bottles and snacks. Always check Care Forms.
VI.   Clean up.
VII. Put all name tags away (on board or in box).

CHILD-CARE FLOOR SUPERVISOR

Note: Depending on the size of your child-care program, this job could be rotated throughout the morning with moms assigned to check on the classrooms at 15 minute intervals throughout the morning (this way no mom has to miss the entire program). However if you have a large number of children's rooms, you might consider making the floor supervisor a hired position who monitors the rooms throughout the entire meeting time.

I.   Check each child-care room throughout the morning.
II.   If a child is upset for 10 minutes, make contact with the mom in the meeting room.
III. Monitor teacher/child ratios in each child-care classroom. Request help from assigned care circle if needed in any classroom.

(Idea: Some groups have found it helpful to provide the child-care workers with Post-it notes they can use to indicate a need for help, or a mother for an upset child, etc. The workers simply jot a note on the sticky paper and place it on the outside of the door. The floor supervisor checks for Post-it notes regularly. This keeps disruptions in the classroom to a minimum.)

CHILD-CARE ROOM MOTHER

One or two mothers per room, one inside the door and one outside the door.

I. Handle problems, comments, and suggestions.
    A. Check with the workers weekly.
    B. Pass concerns to the room mother coordinator for follow-up.
II. Arrive at least 15 minutes before meeting begins.
    A. Fill water pitcher.
    B. Get supply box if necessary.
    C. Pass children from moms to workers.
    D. Go to meeting at 9:05 A.M.
III. Return at the end of meeting to help with pick-up.
IV. Assess clean-up of your room.
    A. Rug vacuumed.
    B. Supplies and toys put away.
    C. Laundry gathered (infant rooms only).
        1. Wash at home.
        2. Return by Friday morning.
    D. Pitcher put away.
    E. Garbage taken out.

Appendix C

Sample Calendars and Schedules

FOR MOMS PROGRAM
SAMPLE ANNUAL PROGRAM SCHEDULE

FALL SEMESTER

SEPTEMBER

23   Welcome Back! Care Circles, Introduction to Group

30   *Topic:* Friendship (and Secret Sister Exchange)

OCTOBER

7   Care Circle Day (includes book review, inexpensive gift, organizational tip)

14   *Topic:* Handling Grief

21   Care Circle Day (includes book review, inexpensive gift, organizational tip)

28   *Topic:* Creative Snack Ideas

NOVEMBER

4   Craft Day

11   Home Business Bazaar

18   *Topic:* Holiday Traditions

25   No Meeting—Happy Thanksgiving!

(If your group hires a lot of college students as child-care workers, you may not want to meet the day before Thanksgiving or during their spring break as many of them leave campus and travel home.)

DECEMBER

2   *Topic:* Keep Jesus the Reason for the Season

9   Holiday Recipe Exchange/Reveal Secret Sisters/Care Circles

SPRING SEMESTER

JANUARY

13   *Topic:* Once a Month Cooking

20   *Topic:* Clear the Clutter

27   *Topic:* Managing Your Money

FEBRUARY

3   Care Circle Day (includes book review, inexpensive gift, organizational tip)

10   Pamper Me Day

17   *Topic:* ABCs of a Healthy Marriage

24   *Topic:* Hearts at Home Video

MARCH

3   Care Circle Day (includes book review, inexpensive gift, organizational tip)

10   *Topic:* The Mommy Monster: Handling Anger Appropriately

17   Silent Auction

24   *Topic:* Breaking the Cycle of Dysfunction

31   No Meeting—Spring Break

(If your group hires a lot of college students, you may need to consider the spring break for the college as well as the break for the local school system.)

APRIL

7   Care Circle Day (includes book review, inexpensive gift, organizational tip)

14   *Topic:* 101 Marriage and Parenting Tips

21   Craft Day

28   *Topic:* TV: The Good, the Bad, and the Ugly

MAY

5   Spring Banquet

SAMPLE CARE CIRCLE HELP SCHEDULE

When your care circle is listed below, we need your help! On the day that you are listed, please plan on assisting with setup, cleanup, child care, and snacks for the moms. Thank you for your help.

FALL

SEPTEMBER

30	Care Circle 1		

OCTOBER

7	Care Circle 2	21	Care Circle 4
14	Care Circle 3	28	Care Circle 5

NOVEMBER

4	Care Circle 6	18	Care Circle 8
11	Care Circle 7	25	No Mom2Mom

DECEMBER

2	Care Circle 9
9	Care Circle 10

SPRING

JANUARY

13	Care Circle 1	27	Care Circle 3
20	Care Circle 2		

FEBRUARY

3	Care Circle 4	17	Care Circle 6
10	Care Circle 5	24	Care Circle 7

MARCH

3	Care Circle 8	24	Care Circle 1
10	Care Circle 9	31	No Mom2Mom
17	Care Circle 10		

APRIL

7	Care Circle 2	21	Care Circle 4
14	Care Circle 3	28	Care Circle 5

MAY

5   Care Circle 6

FOR CHILDREN'S PROGRAM
SAMPLE CHILDREN'S ROOM SCHEDULES

INFANTS AND CRAWLERS

9:00	Free play
10:00	Change diaper
10:15	Snack
10:30	Pick up toys
10:50	Group songs and stories

TODDLERS

9:00	Free play
10:00	Change diaper
10:15	Snack
10:30	Pick up toys
10:50	Group songs and stories

TWO-YEAR-OLDS

9:00	Craft/lesson
9:30	Video
10:00	Bathroom/change diaper
10:15	Snack
10:30	Gym/playground
10:50	Group quiet time/cleanup

THREE-YEAR-OLDS

9:00	Video
9:30	Craft/lesson
10:00	Snack
10:15	Bathroom
10:25	Gym/playground
10:50	Group quiet time/cleanup

FOUR-YEAR-OLDS

9:00	Craft/lesson
9:30	Gym/playground
10:00	Bathroom
10:10	Snack
10:25	Video
10:50	Group quiet time/cleanup

FIVE-YEAR-OLDS

9:00	Gym/playground
9:30	Bathroom
9:40	Snack
10:00	Video
10:30	Craft/lesson
10:50	Group quiet time/cleanup

Appendix D

Sample Forms

SAMPLE MEETING AGENDA WORKSHEET

[To be used by program director or team coordinators.]

Meeting Date _____

Relational Growth (Suggested time: 10 minutes)

_____
_____
_____

Prayer (Suggested time: 15 minutes) (Summarize your prayer approach.)

_____
_____
_____

Vision (Suggested time: 5 minutes)

_____
_____
_____

Spiritual Growth (Suggested time: 10 minutes)

_____
_____
_____

Organizational Growth (Suggested time: 10 minutes)

_____
_____
_____

Team Reports and New Business (Suggested time: 60 minutes)

_____

_____

_____

_____

_____

_____

Prayer (Suggested time: 10 minutes)

_____

_____

_____

Notes:
* Minutes typed _____
* Members not present contacted. (Date) _____

(You may want to email the minutes from your team meeting to all the leadership members. This keeps everyone in communication with each other.)

WORKSHEET FOR CREATING A LEADERSHIP HANDBOOK

[To be used by program director.]

Consider the following elements as you put together a Leadership Handbook.

WELCOME

Sample: Welcome to our leadership team! We trust that this experience will be a memorable venture for you. It is important to communicate how things work in our moms group, so please take the time to familiarize yourself with everything in this handbook. Then communicate this information to your team members, also.

MISSION OR VISION STATEMENT

Sample: Hearts at Home is a nondenominational, professional organization for mothers at home. We desire to exalt God while educating and encouraging women in their personal and family lives.

STATEMENT OF FAITH

Sample: We believe the Bible is the inspired word of God and is held as the final authority on all issues pertaining to the Christian life.

We believe that God exists eternally in three persons—the Father, Son, and Holy Spirit—all being one.

We believe Jesus is God's Son, born of a virgin, fully man yet fully divine.

We believe in Jesus' sinless life, his atoning death through his shed blood, his resurrection from the dead, his ascension to heaven to live with his Father, and his future return to take all believers to heaven for eternity.

We believe in the spiritual unity of believers in Christ Jesus.

We believe that God is active in our lives and he hears and answers prayer.

POLICIES

You might write statements covering issues such as:

- application processes for volunteers

- conduct expectations for leaders or meetings (such as no alcohol at any function or meeting)

- length of leader commitment

- job descriptions

- reimbursement procedures

- conflict resolution procedures (such as Matthew 18 model)

LEADERSHIP EXPECTATIONS

- role of prayer in meetings and in private life
- suggested personal priorities (for example, God, husband, children, church and ministry, other activities)
- guidelines for keeping balance in life
- guidelines for handling difficult situations
- guidelines for facilitating team meetings

SAMPLE BUDGET/FINANCIAL WORKSHEET

Date	Transaction	Deposit		Purchase		Balance	

SAMPLE CORRESPONDENCE DIARY

[To be used by program director or team coordinators.]

Name	Date	Thank You	Appreciation	Other

FOR MOMS PROGRAM
SAMPLE MOM'S REGISTRATION CARD

❏ Check box if this is a new address (for returning moms)

Mom's Name: _____ Husband's Name: _____
Street Address: _____ City: _____ Zip: _____
Phone: _____ Email: _____
Mom's Birthday: _____
Church you attend (if applicable): _____

_____ This is my first time at [name of group].
_____ I am interested in volunteering at [name of group]. Please feel free to contact me.
_____ Please do **NOT** publish my name in the group directory.

We often group our care circles according to similar mothering stages or experiences.
Please check any group that might interest you:
_____ first time moms, children under one year of age
_____ moms of teens
_____ moms who have adopted
_____ moms of special needs children
_____ moms of four or more children
_____ moms of blended families
_____ age of youngest child
_____ age of oldest child

Please list all children in your family:
Name _____ Birth date_____
Name _____ Birth date_____
Name _____ Birth date_____
Name _____ Birth date_____

Please include all of your children's names and ages even if you are not bringing them to the child-care program.
Place a ** next to any child(ren) you will register in the child-care program. Please use our child-care registration form to register your children for our child-care program.

SAMPLE CHILD-CARE REGISTRATION CARD

(Fill out and return only if needing child care)

Mom's Name_____ Phone _____

Mom's Address _____

City_____ Zip _____

Children needing child care:

Name_____ Birthdate_____ Age _____

Name_____ Birthdate_____ Age _____

Will you be bringing children other than your own? _____ Yes _____ No

If yes, list their names and ages:

Name_____ Birthdate_____ Age _____

Name_____ Birthdate_____ Age _____

Are you expecting? _____ If so, when? _____

Child's Doctor_____ Phone _____

Any food allergies? _____

_____

_____

_____

In case of emergency, I give permission for [church's name] to seek medical treatment.

Parent Signature _____

Other Parent Signatures _____
    (for daycare children only)

SAMPLE ATTENDANCE CHART

[May be used for leaders, moms, or children.]

Name	Dates																		

SAMPLE VOLUNTEER SIGN-UP FORM

[This form should be distributed at the end of the year to set up teams for the next year. It should also be given to any new moms who register throughout the year.]

Yes, I would be interested in any of the following teams:

___**Care Circle Leader Team.** Vital to our organization. A leader is in charge of a small circle (15 moms maximum), taking attendance, making new women assigned to the group feel welcome, lining up meals for circle members who may be sick. We could not build friendships very easily without these leaders. (Only one training meeting is required at the beginning of September for this team.)

___**Child-care Team.** Takes care of all aspects of our child care: registration of children, teacher and worker recruitment, snacks, curriculum, etc. Room mothers are part of this team.

___**Craft Team.** Organizes and leads crafts for moms.

___**Facilities Team.** Takes charge of room setup and takedown, refreshment tables, and general atmosphere of our room(s). Works closely with the program team. Perfect for moms with school-age children.

___**Financial Team.** Collects child-care money and activity fees. Makes sure the child-care workers are paid appropriately each week.

___**Hospitality Team.** Team members serve as greeters or "takers" and register new moms each week. Perfect for women who enjoy meeting new mothers.

___**Lending Library Team.** Organizes and maintains a lending library that includes donated books, Hearts at Home audio- and videotapes, magazines, etc. This team will regularly contact book publishers for sample copies of books to help stock the library. It also oversees the checkout process at weekly meetings.

___**Newsletter Team.** Puts together a monthly member newsletter that includes articles by our moms, poems, announcements, and ads. This team will publish and provide finished copies of each newsletter.

___**Program Team.** Selects topics for our weekly meetings, contacts all speakers, organizes discussion groups, etc.

___**Room Mothers.** Each child-care room has one or two room mothers assigned to assist as children arrive and leave. Room moms need to be available 15 minutes before meetings begin. After class they help check kids out. No monthly meetings.

___**Anywhere you need me!**

Check one:

___I am comfortable leading a team. (Commitment includes one leadership meeting a month)

___I prefer to be a committee member. (Commitment includes one committee meeting every other month)

Name _____

Phone _____

MOMS GROUP APPLICATION FOR VOLUNTEER LEADERSHIP

Name _____ Husband's Name _____

Address _____ City _____ Zip _____

Phone _____ Email address _____

Children's names and ages:

Name _____ Age _____

Name _____ Age _____

Name _____ Age _____

Name _____ Age _____

MY TIME RESPONSIBILITIES

1. Do you have a home business? _____

   If yes, how many hours a week does it involve? _____

2. Are you working outside the home? _____ If yes, how many hours per week? _____
   Where are you employed? _____

3. What volunteer positions in church or community organizations do you hold and approximately how much time do they take weekly?

   Organization _____

   Position _____

   Person you report to _____

   Hours weekly _____

4. Would you be willing to give up a volunteer position in another organization to serve in moms group leadership? _____ *Yes* _____ *No* _____ *Not Applicable*

5. Are you in any discipling relationships, small groups, or any other activities that take time outside of your family? _____ If yes, how many hours per week? _____

   Please list specifics: _____

   _____

   _____

6. Looking back over the last 5 questions, how many total hours a week are you involved in activities outside your home? _____

MY SPIRITUAL LIFE

1. Are you comfortable leading a group in prayer? _____

2. Do you attend worship regularly? _____

3. Please share your Christian background and testimony (use back if necessary):

_____

_____

_____

_____

_____

_____

4. How long have you been involved in the moms group? _____

MY PERSONALITY

Please check all that apply. *I am a:*

❒ dreamer   ❒ realist

❒ people manager   ❒ committee leader

❒ delegater   ❒ self-starter

❒ team player   ❒ committee member

❒ lone ranger

Is there anything else you could share that would help us to know you better?

_____

_____

_____

_____

OTHER

1. Are you originally from this area? _____

   If not, where have you lived previously? _____

   _____

2. Do you have a home computer? _____

3. Please list 2 people who would serve as character references for you.

Name _____

Address _____

Phone _____

Name _____

Address _____

Phone _____

SAMPLE SECRET SISTER FORM

Name _____

Address _____ City _____ Zip _____

Birthday _____ Favorite color _____

Favorite pastime or hobby _____

_____

_____

Favorite candy bar _____

Food allergies or dislikes _____

_____

_____

Any other information that will help your Secret Sister know you better?

_____

_____

_____

_____

SAMPLE MIXER FOR A MOMS GROUP

HUMAN BINGO

Find someone who...

Is a twin or a mother of twins.	Sews her own clothes or her children's clothes.	Is at our moms group for the very first time.	Has been to a Hearts at Home conference.	Has been married less than five years.
Was born in another state.	Played sports in high school.	Homeschools.	Has two or more children.	Has an infant less than a year old.
Has lived overseas.	Has a home business.	FREE SPACE	Owns a breadmaker.	Drinks coffee.
Has an artificial Christmas tree at Christmas.	Graduated from the local high school.	Has a wedding anniversary this month.	Has taken at least one college course.	Played an instrument in high school.
Has naturally curly hair.	Has traveled overseas.	Has been married over 15 years.	Has moved to a new home in the past 6 months.	Has adopted a child.

(A person can sign your Bingo card only once!)

Create your own Bingo game:

		FREE SPACE		

SAMPLE PROGRAM EVALUATION

[To be filled out . . .]

Please circle a rating for each area:

Care Circles   Excellent Good   Fair   Poor

Care Circle #_____

Comments: _____

_____

_____

Lending Library   Excellent Good   Fair   Poor

Comments: _____

_____

_____

Child Care   Excellent Good   Fair   Poor

Children's Room Number(s) _____

Comments: _____

_____

_____

Child-care Fees   Excellent Good   Fair   Poor

Comments: _____

_____

_____

Facilities   Excellent Good   Fair   Poor

(Setup and Takedown)

Comments: _____

_____

_____

Craft Days   Excellent Good   Fair   Poor

Comments: _____

_____

_____

Secret Sisters Excellent Good Fair Poor

Comments: _____

_____

_____

Newsletter Excellent Good Fair Poor

Comments: _____

_____

_____

Fundraising Excellent Good Fair Poor

Comments: _____

_____

_____

Please offer any comments on our recent topics and programs. Note which were your favorite and least favorite.

[List your recent topics, programs, events.]

_____

_____

_____

_____

_____

_____

Other Comments

What do you like most about the group? _____

_____

What do you like least about the group? _____

_____

What is your reason for attending this moms group? _____

_____

Do you have topic ideas you'd like to suggest? _____

_____

Do you have craft ideas you'd like to suggest? _____

_____

If you could change something about the group, what would it be? _____

_____

What team would you like to serve on next year?_____

_____

What ideas do you suggest to help our group operate more smoothly? _____

_____

Thank you for your input!

Optional:

Name: _____

Phone: _____

FOR CHILDREN'S PROGRAM
SAMPLE CHILD CAREGIVER APPLICATION

Name: _____

Home Address: _____

Campus Address (for college students): _____

Telephone: _____ Campus phone: _____

Applying for: Teacher or Assistant (circle one)

Please indicate the ages with which you are most comfortable (although we must place you where we most need you, it is helpful to know your preferences):

_____ Infant (0–12 months)

_____ Toddler (1–2 years old)

_____ Preschoolers (3–5 years old)

CPR Certified: _____ Yes _____ No

Other helpful information? _____

_____

_____

_____

Child-care Experience/Classes (List): _____

_____

_____

_____

Church Background: _____

_____

_____

_____

Employment Experience (Past Two Years):

Name of Company/Organization _____

Telephone_____ Position Held _____

Employment Dates (Begin & End, Month & Year) _____·_____

Name of Company/Organization _____

Telephone_____ Position Held _____

Employment Dates (Begin & End, Month & Year) _____

Please List Three Character References (other than relatives):

Name_____Telephone _____

Address _____

Relationship _____

Name_____Telephone _____

Address _____

Relationship _____

Name_____Telephone _____

Address _____

Relationship _____

Have you ever been convicted of a crime (other than a traffic offense)?____ Yes ____ No
If "Yes," please explain on an additional sheet of paper.

Do you have or have you ever been concerned that you may have any past experiences that predisposed you to have a preference that is oriented to children/minors?
_____ Yes _____ No

Have you ever been accused of or charged with committing any act of neglecting, abusing, or molesting any child?_____ Yes _____ No

Were you a victim of abuse or molestation as a minor?_____ Yes _____ No

SAMPLE CHILD-CARE FORM

[For children ages 2 and under. To be filled out by mother and included with diaper bag each week.]

CHILD-CARE FORM

Child's Name _____

Mother's Name _____

Security ID # _____

Please check all that apply

    ❑ Bottle

    ❑ Pacifier

    ❑ Will need nap at _____

    ❑ Allergies

    ❑ Potty Training

Additional information to assist child-care workers in caring for your child _____

_____

_____

_____

_____

SAMPLE CHILD-CARE SECURITY ID TAG

(business card size)

Mom 2 Mom Security ID # 32

This is your permanent ID card for the
Mom 2 Mom childcare program. Please present
this card when picking up your child. This
number is also printed on your child's nametag.

SAMPLE CHILD'S NAMETAG

(business card size)

Austin
Savage
32

Appendix E

Sample Communication

SAMPLE LETTERS FOR LEADERSHIP USE

SAMPLE LETTER TO PROSPECTIVE CHILD-CARE WORKER

Dear Prospective Child-care Giver,

Thank you for requesting an application for employment with our moms group. This group meets weekly and includes a child-care program that runs at the same time as the mothers' program. While the mothers have an opportunity for visiting, hearing guest speakers, sharing ideas, making crafts, or attending a Bible study, the children are playing and learning also.

Our group meets Wednesdays from 9:00 to 11:00 A.M. The first semester begins in September and ends in December. The second semester begins in January and ends at the beginning of May. Child-care workers are needed weekly from 8:15 to 11:30 A.M.

Please completely fill out the enclosed application and return it within the next week to [name and address]. We will notify you for an interview after we review your application.

We know that this is not a lot of hours to work, but it does provide a bit of spending money, and every little bit helps! More important, you will have the opportunity to influence the lives of small children and provide moms with some much needed relief.

Our group meets at [location and address]. Your own transportation is required. Thanks for your interest in our program. We look forward to hearing from you.

Child-care Coordinator

SAMPLE LETTER TO SPEAKER—GUIDELINES

Dear Speaker,

Thank you so much for your willingness to speak to our moms group. We would like to give you a little information to help you plan your message. If you have further questions, please call the contact person listed below. We look forward to our time with you.

Purpose: Our group is a professional, Christian organization for women in the profession of motherhood. We provide weekly social interaction along with teaching on homemaking, marriage, and parenting skills, weaving God's truth throughout all that we do. We are an outreach ministry.

People: You can expect to be speaking to an audience of 100–150 women. Only 40 percent of our regular attendees are members of our congregation. It is an outreach to both the churched and the unchurched.

Handouts and AV Equipment: If you desire to use AV equipment (e.g., VCR/DVD and TV, overhead projector, tape player, PowerPoint), please let [name] know as soon as possible. You will be provided with a microphone. If you want to provide handouts, please have them to [name and maybe place] one week before you speak. Unless you request otherwise, we will have the women pick them up as they walk in the door.

Discussion Questions: We would greatly appreciate 3–5 discussion questions for use in our small groups following your presentation. Please send the questions to [name, address, email] no later than 2 weeks before your visit.

Schedule: Although our schedule varies from week to week, we try to follow this format:

9:00–9:15	Visiting and Food
9:15–10:00	Guest Speaker
10:00–10:15	Break
10:15–10:30	Announcements
10:30–10:55	Small Groups
10:55	Closing Prayer

We ask that you arrive no later than 9:00 A.M., and you are invited to spend the remainder of the morning with us. [Name] will meet you at the receptionist desk at the time you expect to arrive.

Financial Reimbursement: Your honorarium [if any] and travel expenses were determined upon your booking. A check will be given to you on the day that you speak to the group. Thank you for being willing to invest in the lives of mothers and their families by sharing with our moms.

Other: Because this group is an outreach ministry, please refrain from:

- using Christian clichés and phrases (e.g., "saved," "born again") or talking about specific denominations
- highly controversial or political issues
- promoting your project, cause, campaign, or business

Thank you again for sharing with us!

Contact person (program coordinator) _____

Phone numbers_____

Email_____

Date speaking _____

Address and phone of meeting place: _____

_____

_____

[If appropriate attach directions for reaching the meeting place.]

SAMPLE LETTER FOR SUMMER REGISTRATION

[With this letter include registration cards for the mom and the children. This letter can be mailed out to a mom inquiring about the group or it can be handed to a first-time visitor.]

Dear Fellow Mom,

Thank you for your interest in [name of group], a moms group for women in all stages of motherhood. We gather weekly to encourage women in their parenting, their marriages, their homemaking skills, and most of all in their career choice for this season of their lives—mothering. We'd like to introduce you to our program and answer any questions you have.

GENERAL INFORMATION

Our moms group meets each Wednesday morning during the school year from 9:00 to 11:00 A.M. at [name of church]. Children, newborn through kindergarten, may be enrolled in our child-care program at the church for a small fee. There is an activity fee of $10 per semester, which helps pay for program supplies.

CARE CIRCLES

Each woman in our moms group is assigned to a care circle. These groups are organized according to the ages of their children. They allow you to get to know other women who are in a similar stage of motherhood.

CHILD CARE

Our child care allows your child(ren) to play and learn while you are enjoying your two hours at [name of group]. Children 0 to 24 months are cared for according to your instructions. Ages 2 through kindergarten have a curriculum that includes a story/lesson, video, craft, snack, and free play.

CHILD-CARE FEES

Child-care fees are set to cover the costs of running the program while keeping it affordable to one-income families. Fees are payable monthly ($2.50 per child = $10 per month) and are collected on the first week of the month. The maximum child-care fee charged is $6 per family per week ($24 per month). If you are a day-care provider, the same fees will apply to your day-care children, but they will be figured separately from the charge applied to your own children. Child-care fees are nonrefundable and may not be carried over to the next month. If it is financially difficult for you to pay for one month at a time, you also have the option of writing two checks and postdating one for two weeks later. We will then hold that check and deposit it on the later date.

Note: For stay-at-home moms living on one income, money can be tight at times. Please do not ever let money keep you from attending our group. If you cannot afford child care, please contact us to confidentially arrange for scholarship monies. When money is tight, that's usually when we need the support of other moms!

REGISTRATION

You will notice that there are two registration cards, one for you and one for any children you desire to enroll in our child-care program. Please fill out the [pink] card with the requested information about you and your family. Then, fill out the [lavender] card only for the children you want to enroll in child care, including day-care children. Mail them to [name and address].

WAITING LIST

Because our program is so popular, it is possible that some child-care classrooms are at full capacity. If so, we will contact you by phone. If your child is on a waiting list and you can make other child-care arrangements, please do attend the moms program yourself.

DIRECTORY

We publish a moms directory listing the names, children's names, addresses, and phone numbers of all of our members. If for any reason you do not want your address or phone number published, please indicate so on your registration card.

FIRST-TIME ATTENDANCE

When you attend our moms group for the first time, please enter the church building at [give directions to place of meeting]. There you will find women waiting to greet you and introduce you to our program.

I hope this gives you an idea of what our moms group is all about. If you have any further questions, please feel free to give us a call.

We want to encourage you in your mothering. You have made an important choice in staying home and raising your children. No one can replace you! Now let's encourage one another: mom to mom.

[Program director's name]

[Phone]

SAMPLE LETTER TO MOMS ABOUT CHILD CARE

[This letter is included in the registration packet, which could be sent out in a summer mailing or given to moms who register mid-year.]

Dear Mom,

Because leaving a child in child care can sometimes be stressful, we've compiled a list of frequently asked questions to help address concerns or questions you may have.

DO I HAVE TO LEAVE MY CHILD IN CHILD CARE?

Because [name of group] is designed to be a "time out" for mothers, we ask that all mothers use the child-care program or make their own child-care arrangements (newborns up to 6 months can be an exception).

WHAT ABOUT SECURITY?

We have a security system, complete with ID numbers that match you with your child. If your child needs you, your number will be written on the chalkboard. You can excuse yourself to take care of your child's needs, then return to the meeting. You will also need your ID number to pick up your child after a meeting.

WHAT IF MY CHILD CRIES WHEN I DROP HIM OFF?

When you arrive, hang coats in the main hallway upstairs, then go to the child's area and pick up your child's name tag. Take the child to his room. *Please do not enter the child-care room.* This upsets the children already in the room, and it makes it hard to keep track of who is coming and going. Wait at the door for the room mother or teacher to greet you. If your child begins to cry, give him a hug and walk out the door. It may even be necessary for the teacher to "peel" your child off of you. This is a hard thing to do, but most of the time a child stops crying as soon as the parent leaves. If you stick around, it makes it worse for your child, you, and the workers. Allow the workers to do their jobs. They will try very hard to help your child adjust to the room. If your child continues to cry, they will let you know.

WHAT DO I DO IF MY CHILD CRIES IN CHILD CARE?

Let me assure you that not all children cry when their mothers leave them. But should your child cry, we encourage you to give the child-care workers a chance to settle him. If he still doesn't settle down, here are some suggestions for what do to if we come to get you because your child is crying:

1. Tell the floor supervisor you would like to wait 10 to 15 minutes more to give the child a bit more time to settle down.

   Note: We require our workers to inform you when your child has been consistently crying for 10 minutes. We do not necessarily want you to do anything; we just want you to know, give further instructions, or come take care of a need if necessary. You may feel that the child just needs more time to adjust. Let the supervisor know what you want to do. Someone will come to get you again if the child doesn't settle down.

2. Go to the room and help to settle the child down, reassuring him/her that you will come to get them after they are through playing. Work with the child and a worker so that you can exit the room with the child in the care of a specific person. Remember, if they continue to be upset after you leave, we will come get you again.

3. If nothing else works, feel free to bring the child into the meeting with you for that day. Please do not leave to go home. You especially need the morning with other moms after having the stress of an upset child.

WHAT IF I NEED TO NURSE MY CHILD?

If your child needs to nurse, please bring the infant to the moms' meeting room to nurse. That way you won't have to miss the meeting. After you have finished nursing, you can return the child to the child-care room so you can enjoy the rest of the morning.

WHAT IS THE RATIO OF WORKERS TO CHILDREN?

In the infant rooms we try to maintain a 1:2 or 1:3 worker to child ratio. Toddler rooms have a 1:4 or 1:5 ratio. Two- and three-year-old rooms maintain a 1:6 or 1:7 ratio. Our four- and five-year-old rooms have a 1:8 or 1:10 ratio.

CAN I CHECK ON MY CHILD DURING THE MEETING?

We ask that you not go to "check on a child." Once your child or any other child sees an adult, the whole room becomes upset. In the past, our nursery supervisor checked on a room and found all the children happy and playing. Ten minutes later she returned and found several children crying. The workers informed her that a well-meaning mom had peeked in to check on her child, only to upset the whole room. Or the mom had peeked in only minutes after the child had started crying, so she was not aware that the child had just started to cry. The sole job of our nursery supervisor is to walk from room to room making sure that everyone is happy.

If not, she comes to get the mom. By the way, our supervisor doesn't even peek her head in the room. The teachers use Post-it notes on the outside of the door to communicate any problems. This way the room is not disrupted at all.

MAY I TAKE HOME SOME CARE FORMS TO FILL OUT BEFORE WEDNESDAY MORNING?

Yes! It is hard to fill out forms with babies and children in tow. Feel free to grab extra care forms and have them in your child's diaper bag when you arrive (we're enclosing the first one with this letter). Only moms with children 24 months and younger are required to fill out the care forms. You can use your own discretion with 2-year-olds. If your child has a serious allergy or needs special care in any other way, please alert the teacher. We may even make a special note on the child's name tag to assure proper care.

WHAT IF I AM POTTY TRAINING MY CHILD?

We promise to do the best job we can, but please remember that we are caring for multiple children. You may want to use "pull-up" diapers on meeting mornings just to be safe. Two-year-olds on up have "potty breaks," and children are taken to the restroom as they need to be, but we may not catch every child at the right time.

WHAT DO THE CHILDREN DO DURING THE TWO HOURS THEY ARE IN CHILD CARE?

Children 24 months and younger sleep, rock, play, eat, and in general are loved and cared for. Ages 12–24 months have a snack of Cheerios during the morning. Children ages 2 and up have a regular schedule that includes free play, a story, a craft, gym or playground time, and a video every once in a while.

HOW IS DISCIPLINE FOR OLDER CHILDREN HANDLED?

The teachers handle discipline on an individual basis. Sometimes a stern look or a verbal warning is enough. At other times a "time-out" is necessary. When a child consistently misbehaves, the mother will be consulted for further help.

WHAT DO I DO IF I HAVE A CONCERN ABOUT MY CHILD'S CARE OR CLASSROOM?

Please let us know of any concern you have with your child's care. You can speak to the room mother or our child-care supervisor, [name of supervisor]. Please don't just be a complainer. If there is a problem, we need your suggestions too. It may be easier to share your concerns on the phone after you get home rather than with children in tow.

HOW CAN I MAKE THE CHILD-CARE PROGRAM RUN SMOOTHER?

We always need room moms! What does a room mom do? Her biggest job is making the arrival and departure times run as smoothly as possible. She provides extra hands at the most hectic times of the morning. She also maintains regular contact with the teachers and workers in the rooms, passing on needs or suggestions. In the infant rooms, the room moms are responsible for the laundry. It isn't a terribly difficult job, but it is very important. If you are not serving anywhere else in our group, we really need you.

I hope this has answered some of your questions. Please feel free to give me a call [phone number] with any questions or concerns you may have.

[Director's name]

INFORMATION FOR CAREGIVERS

SAMPLE CHILD-CARE WORKER TRAINING SHEET

Church name and location _____

_____

Address _____

_____

Phone number _____

GENERAL INFORMATION FOR CHILD-CARE WORKERS

Discipline: Time-outs may be used if necessary. A chair near the edge of the room should be used to remove the child from activity. State the wrong behavior and tell the child it is not okay. Suggest a good behavior instead. Child may sit one minute for each year of age (3-year-old: 3 minutes). Any recurring problem must be reported to room mother.

Illness: If you have a cold, come anyway. If you have a fever, contagious disease, or serious illness, call [name of person] as soon as possible so we can fill your place.

Ill Child: If the child seems to have a fever, rash, extremely bad cough, or green-mucous runny nose, please notify the floor supervisor.

Crying: When the children arrive, some will cry when they are separated from their mother. It is important that you gently take the child and get him or her interested in something. Do not let the child stand there and cling to Mom. If crying continues, try a walk in the hall or outside. Alert the mom if the child cries constantly for more than 10 minutes.

Rooms: Make sure the rooms are in the same shape or better than you found them. Tell the room mother about any broken toys.

Attendance: You will find weekly attendance charts when you check in. Please be accurate when checking attendance and turn in the chart each week.

Thank you so much for your punctuality, responsibility, and creativity in working with our children.

PARTICIPANTS HANDBOOK

SAMPLE TEXT FOR MEMBERS HANDBOOK

WE WELCOME YOU!

Welcome to our moms group! Being a stay-at-home mom is one of the most rewarding jobs in the world but also one of the most challenging. We all need the support and encouragement of others, and that is why we've come together.

This handbook will acquaint you with the way our group works. Remember, though, this group is your group. We are constantly looking for new ideas to try, new topics to study, new places to go, new crafts to make. . . . If you have any feedback or suggestions, please give them to the appropriate leaders listed below.

Remember that building friendships takes time. Our meetings do not provide enough time to build friendships, but we hope that the care circles will introduce you to women with whom you may choose to build a relationship. We encourage you to get together outside of our meetings. True friendships don't just happen; they take time and effort.

Once again, welcome! We believe you are special. We also believe you have made the right choice to stay home with your children. Join us as we make the journey of full-time homemaking together!

[Director's Name]

OUR LEADERSHIP

This group is made up of women just like you. Please contact any of these women with concerns, questions, or suggestions. We always need more help in all areas! Call [name] today to volunteer!

Women's Ministries

Name_____ Phone_____

Moms Group Program Director

Name_____ Phone_____

Assistant Director

Name_____ Phone_____

Care Circle Coordinator

Name_____ Phone_____

Child-care Coordinator

Name_____ Phone_____

Child Registration Coordinator

Name_____ Phone_____

Craft Coordinator

Name_____ Phone_____

Facilities Coordinator

Name_____ Phone_____

Financial Coordinator

Name_____ Phone_____

Fundraising Coordinator

Name_____ Phone_____

Hospitality Coordinator

Name_____ Phone_____

Lending Library Coordinator

Name_____ Phone_____

Newsletter Coordinator

Name_____ Phone_____

Program Coordinator

Name_____ Phone_____

MONTHLY NEWSLETTER

We have a great monthly newsletter for all you moms, but we need your help to make it the best it can be! You can contribute to the recipe roundup, kids' corner (funny things they say and do, parenting tips, or fun things to do), book and article reviews, and any other information you may need or want to share. There is a newsletter section on our community board in the meeting room; please put your contributions there. For any questions or suggestions call [name].

TRIPS, SLUMBER PARTIES, AND MOMS' NIGHT OUT

Each year we try to plan at least one overnight trip, one slumber party, and several evenings out for moms. Watch for these in the newsletter and during the weekly announcement time. We are also always looking for people to help us organize new activities. Plan to take some time for yourself this year—you deserve it!

LENDING LIBRARY

Please stop by our lending library. The following are some guidelines for its use.

1. You may check out a book/tape/video for 2 weeks.
2. Any items lost or damaged must be replaced.
3. A limit of 5 items may be checked out at any one time.
4. Please return lending library items promptly so others may use them.
5. The lending library will accept donations (not loaned items) anytime during the year.

For further information or questions call [name].

CRAFT DAY GUIDELINES

1. Crafts are offered on a sign-up basis. Sign-ups will be offered at least three weeks before the craft day. The last day to sign up will be two weeks before the craft day.
2. If you sign up for a craft but miss the craft day, you may pick up your pieces and instructions at the next meeting *only*. If you will miss the next meeting, please have someone pick up your craft for you.
3. No refunds will be given for crafts missed.
4. Paint cannot be supplied for crafts that are picked up after craft day.
5. If you miss craft day and forget to pick up your craft the next week, you will forfeit that craft. You cannot expect to "exchange" it for the next craft. This is because the items were purchased and prepared for you even though you did not attend.
6. If you lead a craft, you may participate in one craft being offered that day for free.

Craft days are a favorite for nearly everyone. Because of the number of women we have participating in our group, we have come up with some guidelines to make it easier for all involved. Thank you for your understanding. For those of you not interested in crafts, feel free to bring your own project to work on, or just come and enjoy visiting with other moms for the day. If you would ever like to lead a craft, please see [name].

INCLEMENT WEATHER POLICY

In case of bad weather, our group will follow the local school cancellations. Listen to local radio stations for school closings.

OUR HOSPITALITY AND CARE GROUPS

Because of the size of our group, we have developed a care system that allows moms to get to know one another better and respond to crisis and emergency needs. You will most often meet in your care circle the last 30 minutes of each meeting. This will give you a chance to meet some of the women on a more personal basis. Please, if you have a death in the family, hospitalization, a new baby, etc., call your care group leader immediately. If you cannot get in touch with her or need to find out whose group you are in, call [name]. We want to help one another out in times of stress and trouble, but we have to know the need exists first. For many of us, our moms group is the closest "extended family" we have.

HOME BUSINESS POLICY

Many mothers at home choose to bring in a second income with a home business. We want to be able to give everyone an opportunity to promote her business, but we have established guidelines for marketing a home business at our meetings as follows:

1. No verbal announcements may be made about business specials, parties, or open houses.
2. Our handout table may be used for business handouts and small displays. These need to be removed at the end of each meeting or they will be discarded.
3. Home businesses are welcome to post announcements or brochures on the group's bulletin board.
4. Home businesses are encouraged to participate in our home business bazaar held in November.

CHILD CARE

The child-care program we offer during meetings is set up similar to a preschool.

- Infants through age 2 enjoy interaction, stories, and music.
- They will be cared for according to your instructions.
- Children age 2 through kindergarten enjoy videos, stories, lesson time, crafts, snacks, and playground or gym time.

To help our child care run smoothly, we ask the following from you:

1. When you arrive, please put your child's name tag on the child's back and hand the child to the room mother or worker at the door. Please do not enter the room. The workers are prepared for crying children and will immediately take care of your child. If your child needs you during the morning, someone will come and get you.
2. Please have all items in your diaper bag marked with your child's name (e.g., bottles, pacifiers, cups, etc.). Make sure your diaper bag has your child's name on it too.
3. Fill out a Care Form each week for your child age 2 and under. Feel free to use the same form from week to week, or take a few forms home to fill out when things are less hectic. Turn in your Care Form with the diaper bag.

4. Child care is available from 8:45 to 11:05 A.M. Please be prompt for arrival and pick up.
5. Please notify room mothers of any suggestions or problems. Room mothers will relay the information to the child-care team. The child-care team is striving to make the child-care program the best it can be.

CHILD-CARE FEES

The rate for our child care is $2.50 per child, per meeting. The maximum child-care fee charged is $6 per family. If you are a day-care provider, this policy will apply to your day-care children and must be figured separately from the charge applied to your own children.

Because we realize that dropping off an infant can be difficult, moms with newborns (0–2 months) can have a spot in child care by paying half price for the infant's first month of child care. After that one month, full tuition will be required or the child's spot in the new-born room will be forfeited.

We also realize that you may need some time off after your child's birth. You may pay half tuition for your older children for four weeks if they do not attend. If you attend with your children, then full tuition will be expected.

We require payment of your child-care fees for the entire month at the first meeting of the month. If you are absent that first meeting, you may mail your check or pay your fee the second meeting, or you may lose your spot(s) in the child-care program. The child-care fee is nonrefundable and may not be carried over to the next month. If it is financially difficult for you to pay for one month at a time, you have the option of writing two checks and postdating one for two weeks later. We will then hold that check and deposit it on the later date. You may pay in cash or by check. Checks should be made payable to [organization].

Room mothers should pay their child care first before reporting to their rooms. Please direct any child-care questions to [name].

Please Note: For stay-at-home moms living on one income, money can be tight at times. Please do not ever let money keep you from attending. If you cannot afford child care, please see [name], and she will confidentially arrange for scholarship monies if they are available. When money is tight, that is usually when we need the support of other moms!

OTHER FEES

Our group works under a limited budget, so we ask each mom to share in an activity fee of $10 per semester. This can be paid anytime within the first month each semester. You may also choose to pay for the entire year at once. This fee covers our paper products, child-care supply expenses, and speaker expenses. Once again, if this is a financial problem at all, just let [name] know.

POLICY FOR SICK CHILDREN

If your child has a fever, diarrhea, an unexplained rash, pinkeye, or a green-mucous runny nose, please do not bring the child to the moms group. Your child most likely will not feel like being there and would risk infecting an entire classroom. Thank you for your help in this area.

MOMS' SNACK SCHEDULE

Each care circle will be asked to provide a snack two or three times a year. What do you bring? For moms—anything goes! Finger foods are best. We always provide coffee, tea, cups, plates, and napkins. Please arrive at 8:50 A.M. on the day you provide the refreshments. When it is your circle's day to bring refreshments, each person in the circle should bring something.

CHILD-CARE ROTATION

We want to provide the best care possible for our children, and we are sometimes short-handed in some of the rooms. Because of this, we ask each care circle to be responsible for volunteering in the child-care rooms once per semester. If the teacher indicates that no help is needed, you may attend the program that day. If you really don't want to miss the topic for the day, you may trade with someone else on an individual basis. We appreciate your willingness to help.

PROMOTIONAL COPY

SAMPLE TEXT FOR MOMS GROUP INFORMATIONAL BROCHURE
MEETING THE NEEDS OF MOTHERS AT HOME

WHAT IS [NAME OF GROUP]?

- a haven for frazzled nerves
- an encouraging, accepting atmosphere where a mom finds out she's not alone
- a quality children's program where a mom's little ones are loved and cared for
- a relaxed atmosphere of caring, sharing, and fun

The goal of [name of group] is to nurture all mothers; to reach out with encouragement, friendship, and support; and to enable each woman to be all God created her to be.

TELL ME MORE . . .

Time:	Wednesday mornings from 9:00 to 11:00 A.M. during the school year
Place:	[name of church or building]
Cost:	$10 per semester
Child-care fees:	$2.50 per child per week
Registration:	Please call [phone] for a registration packet

TYPICAL MEETING FORMAT

8:45–9:00 A.M.	Check in children
9:00–9:15 A.M.	Refreshments and conversation
9:15–10:00 A.M.	Speaker
10:00–11:00 A.M.	Care circles

Our group provides quality child care through our child-care program. Children are divided into appropriate age groups. Older children enjoy stories, games, snacks, and songs. Younger children are rocked, held, and cared for according to your instructions.

TYPICAL PROGRAM TOPICS

The ABCs of a Healthy Marriage

Teaching Your Children about God on a Daily Basis

Making Memories with Traditions

101 Ways to Cut Costs: Raising Your Family on One Income

Managing Your Space—Home Organization Ideas

Pamper Yourself: Several businesses will be on hand to do your nails, give you a massage, show you the latest makeup shades, do your colors, and let you try the latest flavored coffee.

For more information call
[name of group]
[name of contact person]
[phone]

Acknowledgments

This book exists because of the efforts of hundreds of moms who have created the moms group they've always wanted and then shared the lessons they learned in the process. In addition to those who shared their stories, special thanks goes to …

… the women of Mom2Mom. You ladies were patient with me as I was learning to be a leader and you loved me in spite of my shortcomings. You also helped create a template for a moms group that hundreds of groups are using today. Thank you!

… the Hearts at Home staff. In the eleven years of Hearts at Home's existence, you have challenged me in my faith and sharpened me as a leader. Thank you for your servant hearts.

… Tonya Irvin, my assistant. Your help in word processing with this book was invaluable to me. Thank you for your encouragement, your prayers, and your servant heart. It's a blessing to do ministry with you.

… my husband, Mark. Finally, we're learning how to navigate the challenges of manuscript deadlines. Thank you for your love, your patience, and your encouragement. Now, sweetheart, this book is really done!

… my children, Anne, Evan, Erica, Kolya, and Austin. You bring a joy to my life that I can't help but want other mothers to experience. Thank you for all that you have taught me in my journey of motherhood.

… Jesus Christ, my Lord and Savior. Thank you for giving me a front row seat to watch you work!

Notes

1. Any other use requires the publisher's permission.
2. Henry T. Blackaby and Claude V. King, *Experiencing God* (Nashville: Lifeway, 1990).
3. Donna Otto, *Mentors for Mothers* (Scottsdale, AZ: self-published, 1999), sec. 2, p. 1.
4. Stormie Omartian, *The Power of a Praying Parent* (Eugene, OR: Harvest House, 1995).
5. Elise Arndt, *A Mother's Touch* (Wheaton, IL: SP Publications, 1983). This book is now only available through the author by phone (248-689-4664) or by email (earndt@faithtroy.org).
6. Bill Hybels, *Too Busy Not to Pray* (Downers Grove, IL: InterVarsity Press, 1988).
7. Ibid., 74.
8. Ibid., 85–95.
9. Ibid. 66.
10. Brenda Hunter, *What Every Mother Needs to Know* (Eugene, OR: Multnomah, 1993).
11. Hearts at Home website, www.hearts-at-home.org, and brochure.
12. Ibid.
13. Ibid.
14. Ibid.
15. Dee Brestin, *The Friendships of Women* (Colorado Springs: Chariot Victor, 1997).
16. Jill Savage, *Professionalizing Motherhood* (Grand Rapids: Zondervan, 2001), 54–58.
17. Neil Anderson, *Victory over the Darkness* (Ventura, CA: Regal, 1990).
18. Brenda Hunter, *What Every Mother Needs to Know* (Eugene, OR: Multnomah, 1993).

Dear Reader,

Thank you for allowing me to share my heart and my stories with you. I hope this book has been helpful to you in your journey to create the moms group you've always wanted. I'd love to hear your stories, your struggles, and your victories within your moms group. I'd also love to hear about your experiences in the profession of motherhood.

Please let me know what was helpful to you in the book. What would you like to hear more about? Did you use The Principles for Successful Leadership section of the book as curriculum for your leadership? If so, was it helpful? Did you download any of the appendixes off the website? If so, were they helpful? I look forward to hearing your thoughts!

I can be reached personally by:

Mail: c/o Hearts at Home
          900 W. College Ave.
          Normal, IL 61761
Email: jillannsavage@yahoo.com
Website: www.jillsavage.org
          www.hearts-at-home.org

My speaking schedule is posted on my website—who knows, I may be coming to your area! If so, I'd love to meet you!

May God bless you on your parenting journey, and may he always keep your heart at home.

Joining you in the journey,
Jill

Available Online!

You can download all job descriptions, forms, and letters listed in the appendixes of this book! This will save you time because you will not have to begin from scratch. Simply go to www.jillsavage.org. Click on Moms Groups and enter this password in the box provided: HeaRt4Home

You can now have the information on your computer to edit and personalize for your group!

Hearts at Home®

The Hearts at Home organization is committed to meeting the needs of women in the profession of motherhood. Founded in 1993, Hearts at Home offers a variety of resources and events to assist women in their jobs as wives and mothers.

Find out how Hearts at Home can provide you with ongoing education and encouragement in the profession of motherhood. In addition to this book, our resources include the *Hearts at Home* magazine, the *Hearts at Home* devotional, and our Hearts at Home website. Additionally, Hearts at Home events make a great getaway for individuals, moms groups, or for that special friend, sister, or sister-in-law. The regional conferences, attended by over ten thousand women each year, provide a unique, affordable, and highly encouraging weekend for the woman who takes the profession of motherhood seriously.

Hearts at Home
900 W. College Ave.
Normal, Illinois 61761
Phone: (309) 888-MOMS
Fax (309) 888-4525
Email: hearts@hearts-at-hom.org
Website: www.hearts-at-home.org

Would you like additional resources for your group?

We hope your moms group is growing and thriving. If you would like to provide your group additional mothering resources, make a copy of the form below, fill in the information on the copy, and mail or fax it to Hearts at Home. Your sample resources (magazine, devotional, and more!) are free of charge and will arrive within 3–6 weeks. (The form is also available on our website.)

Additionally, Hearts at Home maintains a comprehensive database of moms groups in the United States. This allows us to operate as a clearinghouse for information about the groups. For instance, if a woman moves to a new community, she can contact Hearts at Home to locate a group in her area. If you would like to be part of the Moms Group Referral Network, please indicate below as well.

❒ Yes! Please send me resources for my group!

Please ship to:

(Name of group) _____

(Name of leader) Attn: _____

(Shipping address) _____

City_____ State_____ Zip _____

(Contact name and phone number)_____

(Contact email) _____

How many women regularly attend your group? _____

☐ Yes! Please include our group in your referral network!

Name of group _____

Meeting address _____

City_____ State_____ Zip _____

Contact name and phone number _____

Group email (if applicable) _____

Group website (if applicable) _____

Hearts at Home
900 W. College Ave.
Normal, Illinois 61761
Phone: (309) 888-MOMS
Fax (309) 888-4525
Email: hearts@hearts-at-home.org
Website: www.hearts-at-home.org

Professionalizing Motherhood

Encouraging, Educating, and Equipping Mothers at Home

Jill Savage, Founder and Director of Hearts at Home®

"Just a mom?" There's no such thing. Motherhood isn't a second-rate occupation. It is a career that can maximize your talents and strengths to their fullest. Look past the surface of mothering—the endless tasks and frantic pace—to the incredible skills required to raise your children and nurture your marriage. The truth is clear: You're a professional in one of the most dignified, demanding, and rewarding fields any woman can find.

Upbeat, candid, and engaging, *Professionalizing Motherhood* will do more than help you radically redefine how you see yourself. It will guide you toward practical development as a career woman who specializes in the home. Jill Savage helps you determine a strategy and set goals for professional training and growth. From the foundational to the practical, you'll learn about

- Establishing the mission of your job
- Developing a network of "coworkers"
- The all-important foundation of knowing your value in Christ
- How marriage and mothering work together
- Organizational and homemaking basics
- Taking care of your personal needs
- And much more

Professionalizing Motherhood casts a fresh and meaningful vision for mothering as a worthy career choice for this season of your life. Get ready to be inspired as you discover how profoundly meaningful and influential a profession motherhood is.

Softcover: 0-310-24817-5

Pick up a copy today at your favorite bookstore!

ZONDERVAN™

GRAND RAPIDS, MICHIGAN 49530 USA

WWW.ZONDERVAN.COM

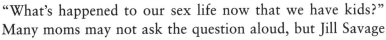

Becoming a Chief Home Officer

Thriving in Your Career Shift to Stay-at-Home Mom

Allie Pleiter

Allie Pleiter knows firsthand the culture shock, surprises, joys, and uncertainties of leaving the workplace to stay at home and raise children. With disarming wit and a refreshing personal transparency, Pleiter tackles both the "whys" and "hows" of this transition that strike at the very core of a woman's concept of self, of accomplishment, of worth. *Becoming a Chief Home Officer* constructs a fresh new "benefits package" for the profession of motherhood and offers a wide array of practical advice from "labor relations" in averting strikes and tantrums, to new perspectives in seeking "raises, praises, and promotions."

Three distinct audiences will find help and hope in these pages: the working woman considering this transition, the newly-at-home mom adjusting to culture shock, and the "approaching burnout," been-home-awhile mom struggling with frustration or dissatisfaction. Pleiter's witty admission of mistakes and mishaps evokes knowing grins and empathetic laughter to punctuate her wonderfully practical advice.

Softcover: 0-310-23742-4